MYRNA and ROBERT KYSAR have combined their experience in counseling and their expertise in biblical studies to produce this fine study of divorce and remarriage according to the Scriptures. Myrna Kysar has seven years' experience in the parish as an ordained minister doing pastoral and marital counseling. She received her Master of Divinity from Yale Divinity School. Robert Kysar, noted New Testament scholar and author of JOHN, THE MAVERICK GOSPEL (John Knox Press), is Professor of Religion at Hamline University in St. Paul.

THE ASUNDERED

THE ASUNDERED

Biblical Teachings on Divorce and Remarriage

*"Those whom God has joined together,
let no one put asunder."*
Mark 10:9

by
Myrna and Robert Kysar

JOHN KNOX PRESS
ATLANTA

THE ASUNDERED

Scripture quotations marked "NEB" are from *The New English Bible,* copyright ©
by The Delegates of The Oxford University Press & The Syndics of The Cambridge
University Press 1961, 1970. Reprinted by permission.

Scripture quotations marked "RSV" are from the Revised Standard Version Bible,
copyright 1946, 1952, and © 1971, 1973 by the Division of Christian Education of the
National Council of the Churches of Christ in U. S. A. and are used by permission.

Scripture quotations marked "Good News Bible" are from the Good News Bible: The
Bible in Today's English Version, © 1976 by the American Bible Society, and used by
permission.

Scripture quotations marked "KJV" are from the King James Version of the Holy
Bible.

Unmarked Scripture translations are by the authors.

Library of Congress Cataloging in Publication Data
  Kysar, Myrna.
    The asundered.

    Bibliography: p.
    Includes indexes.
    1. Divorce—Biblical teaching. 2. Remarriage—
  Biblical teaching. I. Kysar, Robert,
  joint author. II. Title.
HQ824.K9   301.8'34'284   77-79591
ISBN 0-8042-1096-9
© 1978 John Knox Press

Printed in the United States of America

ACKNOWLEDGMENTS

The original inspiration for this book came a number of years ago as we were confronted in a very direct way with the importance of the ministry of the church to divorced and sometimes remarried persons. That original inspiration grew into a plan as we involved ourselves in various ways in the life of the community of faith. The final determination to write the book was an effort to bring together our mutual experiences and skills into the kind of a volume we hope will prove helpful to both clergy and interested lay people in the church. But clearly it was the individual Christians who went through the experience of divorce and our commitment to the ministry of the church that formed the beginning point of our project.

Along the way during the past four years any number of persons have contributed in an indirect way to this volume. We think in particular of Professor Rowan Greer of Yale Divinity School, Professor Mark Hillmer of Northwestern Lutheran Theological Seminary, and Mr. Gregory Bancroft, a Yale seminarian. They each contributed in a formative way to the shaping of the treatment of the Biblical passages considered in this book. But we must mention, too, the numerous persons who have encouraged our effort and have confirmed our conviction that such a book as this is needed. To all of them we issue here our thanks and our acknowledgment of their help.

But most especially we want to thank those "asundered" of our society who with determination have clung to the church through their painful life transition. They have with courage and conviction helped us all to practice what this book is intended to nurture, and by their lives they have doubtless done more to enhance the ministry of the church to the divorced and sometimes remarried than we can ever hope to do. It is to those persons we dedicate this book.

CONTENTS

CONTENTS

Introduction
The Asundered and the Church

The decision to file for divorce was very difficult for Janice and Dick. They had been married for twelve years, but their marital problems had haunted them from the very first months of their marriage. Somehow during their courtship they had failed to see the problems that awaited them in their marriage. To be sure, there had been some good times. But the conflicts had come and gone only to come again. Steadily those conflicts intensified as the years wore on. Try as they could, there seemed to be no peace for them together. They would quarrel and the days of alienation would follow. Then there would be a reconciliation with a new determination to do better. But too soon the conflicts would arise again and the resolutions to do better would be crushed under the pressure of what appeared more and more to be irreconcilable differences.

Their counseling had begun in the fifth year of their marriage. The birth of their child had brought a crisis too severe to bear. Janice had secretly hoped that the baby would draw her and Dick closer together, but instead the opposite happened. First, they went to their pastor and after a time he had referred them to a private psychologist. Dick and Janice were determined to make their marriage work. They would spare no expense to get the kind of help they needed. The counseling went on and on. They met with the therapist as individuals; they met with her as a couple; and they tried other counselors with different techniques. They even participated in group therapy for several years. New insights came, but so often the insights would not result in easing the increasing tension in the marriage. Instead, the insights into their respective personalities only seemed to heighten the problem. Their backgrounds were so different, their life-styles and values at such variance, and their personalities so opposite that it seemed hopeless.

But Dick and Janice would not give up their hope of achieving a workable marriage.

Divorce was abhorrent to them both. They had been raised in the church, and both were convinced that divorce was wrong. Dick had gradually dropped out of the activities of the church as his marital problems grew in intensity. He said that it made him feel like a hypocrite to go to church only to engage in a furious argument with Janice on Sunday evening over some trivial matter. They had discussed divorce many times—sometimes rationally, sometimes very emotionally. But both were reluctant. Not only did they view divorce as religiously offensive, but they knew a divorce would hurt their parents deeply. And what would their friends think?

One night during a terrible quarrel, Richie, their eight-year-old son, came out of his room rubbing his sleepy eyes and pleading through his tears, "Please, Mommy and Daddy, don't fight anymore. Don't you like each other?" Shocked into rationality by the simple but impassioned words of their son, Janice and Dick faced the fact that they did *not* like one another. Neither would choose the other as a friend. How could they go on living together behind a facade of wife and husband? And now they had to acknowledge what they had tried to deny before: their conflicts were scarring the life of their son.

The divorce was quiet and amicable. Dick moved to another part of town and would see Richie regularly. But Janice felt a terrible and intense fear. She was alone for the first time in her life. What would she do? How could she survive as a single woman with a child?

A month after the divorce Janice went back to church. She was frightened and embarrassed. She bore an unimaginable burden of guilt, for she could not escape the feeling that she had failed miserably. But just because she was frightened, lonely, and guilty she thought that she should return to her church. She knew she needed that supportive fellowship more now than anytime in her life. But what a strange experience it was returning to her church. The Russells—with whom she and Dick had had a friendly relationship—avoided her; they went quickly out the side exit immediately after the service. Old Mrs. Smith, who used to talk with Janice interminably during the coffee hour following the worship service, this Sunday only smiled and walked past. Janice seemed to sense only coldness everywhere. The official "greeters" did their duty, but Janice felt no warmth in their welcome. Even the pastor seemed embarrassed and at a loss for words. It occurred to Janice that she was imagining all of this. Perhaps because she felt so self-conscious, she was twisting everything others did into indications of rejection. Maybe her own feelings of guilt were filtering out all of the positive, accepting, and consoling actions and words and letting through only messages of rejection. But Richie had fared no better at church school. He reported that his teacher had said something about how it was too bad his parents had gotten a divorce and that perhaps if they had had more faith in God it would not have happened.

Janice, however, was determined. She needed the church. So she went back to choir practice and later that week attended the women's meeting. But the feeling of coldness and rejection persisted. Everything was different. She did not seem to fit any longer. In desperation she went to see the pastor. He was very kind and understanding. He suggested that people did not intend to reject her, but that they were clumsy and did not know the right words to say. He gently but clearly offered what Janice had suspected, namely, that her own guilt was getting in the way of her relationship with people of the congregation. He proposed that the difficulty Janice was experiencing was due to a number of complex reasons: To be sure, some of the people in the congregation were prejudiced against divorce, and from them there would be rejection. Others were just at a loss as to how they should relate to Janice. And finally Janice herself was part of the problem. Janice had to admit that what the pastor said was true, and her visit with him helped a good deal. She was, however, so uncomfortable that when the pastor suggested that she come back for another discussion of her feelings, she declined.

But she did continue for a time to go to church. Gradually, however, she began dropping out. She could not overcome the terrible discomfort she felt among the members of the congregation. The loss of her church only increased her anger—now she had lost not only her husband but her church as well. Not only had he rejected her; she felt rejected, too, by Christians. Janice never returned to her church. She looked elsewhere for the fulfillment of her needs. Eventually she became a member of a group of divorced persons unrelated to the church. They supplied some of the fellowship she needed to deal with her loneliness. She sought out a therapist and there tried to resolve the feelings of guilt which she felt that the church had not helped her handle.

It is a common story. The tragedy of a broken marriage is made more tragic by a broken relationship with the church. Must the church and the divorced turn their backs on one another? Must it be this way? Can the church not minister to the asundered of our society? Must the commitment to the conviction that divorce is a sin, the clumsiness of Christians in the presence of divorced persons, and the tremendous burden of guilt that accompanies divorce alienate those who suffer marital breakdowns? How can the Biblical teachings regarding divorce and remarriage be understood so as to enhance the ministry of the church to these people?

The premise of this book is that Janice's experience with the church need not be the norm. The church's ministry to the divorced of our society can be more creative and helpful. It need not be condemnation and rejection. The Biblical teachings upon which the church depends for guidance do not necessitate that the church add its condemnation to that of society.

Needless to say the problem of divorce plagues the church and our whole society more and more each year. More and more pastors are faced with divorces in their congregations and are increasingly confronted with divorced persons seeking the blessing of the church upon a second marriage. And, increasingly, divorce is haunting the ranks of the clergy too. Local congregations and church officials are asking what they are to do with divorced members of the clergy who desire to continue in the ministry. We could cite statistics. But doubtless by the time you had read them here they would be out of date and the figures actually much higher.

The problem posed for the church and devout Christians is a serious one. Do we capitulate to the growing ease with which divorce is being accepted today as a common phenomenon? Do we silence our protest against this rampant tragedy that is breaking up families and causing such widespread pain? Yet if we continue to protest and condemn divorce for the tragedy it is, how can we minister effectively to the hurt and pain of divorced persons who, like Janice, turn to the church? Those passionate and loving Christians concerned and informed about this problem feel as though they are dangling from the two widely separated horns of an irresolvable dilemma.

Our purpose here is to ask if there is a way out of this dilemma. We propose that it is time for the church to take a new look at the Biblical teachings on divorce and remarriage and ask what those teachings say to the ministry of the church. So what we will attempt to do is investigate the Biblical teachings once again. This time we will examine those passages on divorce and remarriage critically and carefully. We want to ask what light contemporary Biblical scholarship can throw on those teachings. It should be noted from the beginning that ours is neither an apology for divorce nor an attack upon it. We do not propose to defend any thesis but one: that it is time for a reassessment of the Biblical teachings on divorce and remarriage in the light of critical scholarship. We know that there are some misunderstandings of those teachings among some Christians, both lay and clerical. But ours is not the task to try the impossible, namely, the defense of divorce and remarriage on Biblical grounds. All we ask is that you come to this study with as open and critical a mind as possible, and together we will see what happens.

It must also be noted that this study is but a modest contribution to the effort to understand divorce and remarriage from a Christian perspective. This book cannot claim to answer all of the questions or articulate all the insights we need today for the ministry of the church in this troublesome area. As we will point out there is a good deal of theological reflection needed, especially with regard to the whole institution of marriage. There is an equal need for the articulation of all of the best psychological insights into marriage, divorce, and remarriage from the perspective of Christian faith. Moreover, sociological analyses of the effect of divorce and remarriage must be studied. All of these are needed for an informed, effective ministry to the fact of divorce and remarriage in our society and to the persons involved in that fact. If this book makes a contribution at all, and we believe it does, it is at the point at which the church's reassessment of this problem must begin, but not end—the Biblical foundations.

The goal of this book is therefore twofold: first to investigate the Biblical teachings on divorce and remarriage in the light of the best modern scholarship and, second, to apply that investigation to the ministry of the church. Our attempts to achieve these goals will, we hope, provide a way of beginning the process of discussion of the issue. The beginning of any good discussion is when someone offers a statement which she or he believes has some validity. The subsequent discussion may move considerably beyond the original statement, but that statement provides the stimulation and the basis for further conversation. We invite you, the reader, to use this book as that kind of initial discussion starter—a discussion that eventually leads Christians individually and as a church to a more positive and vital role in the ministry to divorced and remarried persons in our society.

Several other things need to be said before we begin our investigation of the Biblical material. We will place Scripture passages in the context of what modern Biblical interpreters regard as the necessary ingredients for good exegesis. Consequently, the following three chapters will be concerned with historical, literary, contextual, and other critical kinds of questions regarding each of the major passages dealing with divorce and remarriage. The pragmatic reader may be tempted to ask how some of this is important for the immediate question of the ministry of the church. We can only respond by insisting that the Biblical foundations of the church's ministry must always be the result of the best critical insights available. An indispensable premise of this book is that critical Biblical scholarship is not only a friend of the church's ministry but an ally without whose help the church is bound to become misdirected.

But our study of the relevant passages includes the risky business of hermeneutics as well—the fine art of interpretation. When we ask from our twentieth-century perspective how a Biblical passage, written perhaps as long as 2600 years ago, is relevant to our Christian lives, a great deal is involved. The way we have posed our question to the texts will be influential. The presuppositions of the culture in which the texts were written and the culture out of which the interpreter thinks will both shape what is concluded. We enter this process of interpretation with fear and trembling, for we are acutely aware of how vulnerable the interpreter always is. But it is just this risk that the Christian must always take—the risk of being wrong or only partially right. With an awareness of this risk, it is our hope that the reader will try to maintain an openness to truth, as we have tried to remain open.

Finally, we have assumed that there is still some validity in the Christian conviction that the canon of the Bible offers the church its guideposts. It is not that the Biblical material is the last word to be spoken on any question. Nor is it the case that the Biblical teachings must always be taken as absolutely normative for the Christian. The Word of God continues to address twentieth-century persons through the words of the Bible; but the Word of God is never identical to those words of the Bible. Those human words are instruments, tools, media through which the message may come into our contemporary situations. Yet they remain human words to be studied as such, except that they must be studied with a constant awareness of their potential to become the divine Word. So we have approached those Biblical words armed with our tools of criticism but also with a certain respect as well. Because we are committed to the canonical place of the Bible in the Christian church, we have put to one side the question of the insights of post-Biblical material. A profitable study would surely be the investigation of the history of divorce and remarriage in Jewish and Christian thought since the Biblical era. But it is not the profit of that study that we seek.

Actually the guideposts for the ministry of the church to divorced and possibly remarried persons are few in the Biblical witness. We have isolated the major sayings in the Old Testament, in the Gospels, and in the epistles for our study. From these we have tried to draw conclusions that are in the spirit of the entire Biblical witness to God's revelatory activity in the history of the Hebrew and Christian communities. Whether our investigations and our conclusions are sound, you are asked to decide for yourself. But on this much we must agree now: the need for a reassessment of the Biblical teachings on divorce and remarriage for the ministry of the church is urgent.

1

MOSES' PERMISSION
Divorce and Remarriage in the Old Testament

The Christian stands on one main branch of what may be visualized as a large tree with two major branches. The one branch is the Christian movement; the other is Judaism. But both branches of our imaginary tree have a common trunk. That trunk is, of course, the Hebraic faith. And that faith is given expression in what Christians have come to call the Old Testament. In a sense, the literature of the Old Testament is as much a part of the heritage of the Christian faith as it is a part of the heritage of the modern Jew. To be sure, the Jews and the Christians view that literature differently. For the Jew it is viewed from the perspective of centuries of a process of interpretation, found in part in the ancient Mishnah and the Talmud. The Christian, on the other hand, views the literature of the Hebraic faith through the glass of the revelation of God in Christ. But the Old Testament literature must be taken by the Christian, as by the Jew, as the record of the very early conviction that God was at work in a special way among a group of people, revealing to them his nature and will. Very early, the Christian church declared that it would not disown its roots in the Hebraic faith. The church declared that to do so was a heretical distortion of the true character of Christian faith. Hence, when we ask what the founding revelation of God was for the beginning of our tradition, we must turn first to the Old Testament.

The task is not an easy one, however. For the Old Testament is a complex collection of literature arising out of the history of a people over a period of nearly a thousand years. Moreover, the revelation of God witnessed to in that literature is encased within a cultural perspective. The revelation of God is never received in the abstract. Rather, it is perceived by persons living within the confines of a culture and that culture's presuppositions and assumptions regarding truth. The revelation comes therefore into a concrete and specific cultural situation. That is the very nature of the historical revelation so central to Judaism and Christianity. The clothes a person wears are made to suit that person's body. But at the same time the clothes themselves shape the person's body, sometimes even conceal the true nature of that body. To examine a physical body, the clothes must be removed. Similarly, to examine the revelation of God given expression in the Old Testament, we must recognize that it both shapes and is shaped by its cultural clothing. In any case, the interpreter of the Old Testament must attempt to remove that cultural clothing, however reverently and carefully.

When we turn to the Old Testament to ask what it says about the issues of divorce and remarriage, we find a number of different kinds of passages. There are, first of all, *legislative passages* that prescribe regulations for divorce and remarriage. In Leviticus (22:13), there are laws regarding the right of the daughters of priests to return to their fathers after a divorce. And in Leviticus 21:14, priests are forbidden to marry divorced women. Laws concerning the vows a woman may take and in what cases they are binding include the vows of a divorced woman (Num. 30:9). Deuteronomy 22:19, 28-29 forbids divorce in cases where a man has slandered his wife and in cases where a man has seduced a virgin and is forced to marry her. The primary divorce and remarriage law, however, is found in Deuteronomy 24:1-4, and it is upon that passage we will eventually focus our attention.

Second, there is a *prophetic passage* which decries the frequency of divorce among the Hebrew people. Malachi 2:13-16 declares that the ease with which divorce is practiced is an insult to God. In verse 16 of this passage the prophet says that the divorces of his day are objectionable because of the cruelty they inflict upon women. In this verse we hear a theme which anticipates much that we find in the Old Testament on the subject of divorce and remarriage. It is concerned not so much to prohibit divorce as to minimize the cruelty that results from the practice.

Third, there are a large number of *metaphorical passages,* especially in the prophets, where divorce is used as an analogy for the relationship of God to the people of Israel. Jeremiah 3:1-8 is one such example, and Isaiah 50:1 another. The most famous passage of this kind, however, is found in the prophet Hosea, chapters 1—3. There

God's justice demands that he "divorce" the "unfaithful wife," Israel. But his love and mercy equally demand that he be reunited with her. In every case these passages do not add to our understanding of the practices of the Hebrew people so much as they take for granted the practice of divorce in that culture.

All these passages demonstrate one thing quite clearly. Divorce was a common practice in Hebraic society of Old Testament times. The legislative passages, the prophetic passage in Malachi, and the analogical passages imply that divorce was a culturally accepted phenomenon. There were efforts to control it in specific situations (e. g., Lev. 21:14), but it was frequent enough to be used as a common metaphor. Nowhere in the Old Testament do we find legislation that prohibits divorce for the ordinary lay person. Divorce is taken for granted. What the legislation and Malachi's prophetic declaration attempt to do is control divorce in such a way as to humanize the practice. The Old Testament, we may say in general, is concerned that divorce and remarriage be done in the most humane way possible.

It is, of course, the passage in Deuteronomy 24:1-4 which is the center of attention among the various Old Testament passages on these subjects. This is so, perhaps, because it appears to have the widest application and was taken to be the general position of the Torah on the questions under consideration. For Christians this passage emerges as most important, for it is the one that Jesus cites in his teaching on divorce and remarriage. (See the next chapter.) So we will attempt a careful study of the legislation found in Deuteronomy 24:1-4 as the heart of the Old Testament teaching on our subject.

The Deuteronomic Legislation on Divorce and Remarriage

Let us begin our descent into the verses in Deuteronomy from a lofty elevation. We must first ask ourselves what the practices of the other ancient Near Eastern countries were regarding divorce. But in this case, the study of other cultural practices of the time does not enlighten the passage in Deuteronomy a great deal. While some Old Testament law evidences influence from the practices of other cultures of the time, there is little influence exhibited in the areas of divorce and remarriage. As a matter of fact, most scholars recognize that other cultures show a greater degree of sensitivity to the issues involved in divorce than the Old Testament does. The Code of Hammurabi, for instance, witnesses to Babylonian practices stemming from as early as 1700 B.C. The laws on divorce in that ancient code are more detailed and specific than one can find anywhere in the Old Testament. They provide, for instance, that the man pay a price to the woman he divorces, and under certain circumstances they even allow a woman to divorce her husband. (See *Ancient Near Eastern Texts Relating to the Old Testament,* ed. James B. Pritchard [Princeton, N.J.: Princeton University Press, 1950], p. 172. See also John Paterson, "Divorce and Desertion in the Old Testament," *Journal of Biblical Literature* 51 [1932]: 161-170.) In some ways it appears that other cultures had what we might call a more humane and elaborate body of divorce legislation than the Hebrew people did. However, nowhere in other ancient Near Eastern legal literature do we find a prescription quite comparable to that found in Deuteronomy 24:1-4.

Deuteronomy represents a legal document which dates, most likely, from the seventh century in the Southern Kingdom of Judah. It doubtless has roots that go back much earlier, and scholars have sought to discover those roots. Some believe that its origins were actually in the Northern Kingdom at least as early as the eighth century. This view is held for the most part because the book reflects little if any specific concern for the Southern Kingdom itself and its peculiar interests. Missing, for instance, is the emphasis upon the Davidic tradition that was so much valued by the Southern Kingdom of Judah. Moreover, the parallels between Deuteronomy and the book of the prophet Hosea have been taken as evidence that the former took its original shape in the Northern Kingdom in the eighth century. On the other hand, most scholars identify the book of Deuteronomy or some portion of it with the "book of the covenant" discovered a century later in Jerusalem. It was doubtless one of the things that inspired King Josiah to undertake a widespread religious reform in 621 (2 Kings 22—23).

As a whole, the book of Deuteronomy presents itself as the farewell sermon of Moses, although it is obvious that it was directed toward the people of Israel at a much later date. Its purpose seems to be to make old cultic and legal traditions relevant to its readers. The style of the book is homiletic, even though it is made up of different kinds of materials. As a matter of fact, the Old Testament scholar Gerhard von Rad has called the book a "mosaic of innumerable, extremely varied pieces of traditional material" (*Deuteronomy: A Commentary* [Philadelphia: The Westminster Press, 1966], p. 12). He sees essentially four parts to the book as a whole: first, a historical survey with exhortations (chapters 1 through 11); second, a body of legal material (12:1—26:15); third, a covenant statement (26:16-19); and, fourth, a series of blessings and curses (chapters 27 through 30). Von Rad demonstrates that the whole of the book shows signs of having gone through a long process of development before reaching its present literary form. He suggests that the basic harmony of the book as a whole lies in its general homiletic tendency. There is a single style that permeates all of the book's material—historical, legal, and all the rest. But let us move closer to the verses that are our specific concern by focusing now upon the legal materials in Deuteronomy.

If von Rad is correct, the laws in Deuteronomy reflect a liturgical setting—that is, a setting of worship. They have been preached over and over again in the context of a worship service. In the process of their restatement in worship, they have been developed gradually into the form in which they present themselves in Deuteronomy. Moreover, they are set in Deuteronomy within the context of the covenant and the renewal of the covenant relationship. Within the liturgy that must have been the early home of the Deuteronomic legal material the covenant was a recurring central theme. Hence, we might say that what binds the laws together in this book, in addition to the homiletic style in which they are presented, is their common basis in the covenant.

Perhaps at this point an illustration will help. Suppose someone were to collect a series of modern exhortations on such contemporary issues as, say, world hunger, racial equality, the rights of women and minority groups, the need for morality in the contemporary business world, etc. These might be gathered from sermons preached in American pulpits over the past decade. That collection would betray to the careful reader some common themes and tone. The style in every case would be homiletical. Implicit in the exhortations would be the fact that they were declared within a setting of worship. Moreover, the careful student of our hypothetical collection would probably pick up again and again its context: the Christian gospel. Sometimes that context would be explicit in the exhortations themselves; sometimes it would be only implied. Our analogy suggests the way in which the legal material of Deuteronomy may be studied. Those laws, too, have their setting in worship; they are sermonic in tone; and they betray a conceptional environment centered in the covenant (as our hypothetical collection betrays a setting in the gospel).

We can push our analysis of the laws of Deuteronomy a bit further. We note as we study those laws carefully that there are two distinct types. There is first of all the *absolute* (or *apodictic) law form.* These are straightforward "you shall" and "you shall not" laws. Examples most readily at hand include the Decalogue (5:6-21) and a passage like 14:3-20. In these cases, a command is stated in such a way as to suggest that it is always applicable. "You shall not commit adultery." (5:18, NEB) No condition or situation is described; the absolute regulation is simply announced. Von Rad has argued that such laws had their original home in the cultic setting. There God is understood to speak directly and absolutely in the law. The modern-day parallel might be the Christian preacher exhorting, "We must love and care for those our society regards as social outcasts!"

The second form of law in the book of Deuteronomy is the *conditional law.* In this case, the prohibition follows a statement of a situation. The law is called "conditional" because it is based upon the existence of some set of circumstances. Examples in the book of Deuteronomy abound. Let us take only one as a model: "When you reap the harvest in your field and forget a swathe, do not go back to pick it up; it shall be left for the alien, the orphan, and the widow, in order that the LORD your God may bless you in all that you undertake." (Deut. 24:19, NEB) The law first of all states a very definite situation or condition: you are harvesting, and you miss some portion of the field. When that happens, you are commanded not to go back and harvest that row, but leave it for the needy. Such conditional, or we might call them situational, laws are more specific in a sense, for they exhort specific behavior in a specifically described situation. The absolute laws, on the other hand, are more general. Conditional legislation calls to mind the legal assembly. Scholars argue that these laws took their origin in a setting where legal decisions are being made. They sound in some ways like the decision written by a judge after having heard a case argued. But the legal setting has been left behind in the development of the laws of this kind in Deuteronomy, as is suggested by the concluding clause in our example above. Tacked on to the conditional law about leaving the unharvested swathe in the field is a "motivational clause"—"in order that the LORD your God may bless you in all that you undertake." The law is made now into a religious exhortation. This kind of conditional law might also find its parallel in the preaching of the contemporary pastor. "If ex-convicts come to us seeking membership in our church, and if they demonstrate sincere desire to be a part of our community and embrace the Christian life, we must receive them gladly." And the preacher too might add a motivational clause: "For this is precisely the spirit of acceptance we see in the life of Jesus as he related to those of his day who were social outcasts."

The passage contained in Deuteronomy 24:1-4 is obviously a law stated in "conditional form." It has been called a "pure conditional law," for the situation is described without parenthetical breaks of any kind. But therein lies one of the first problems we must deal with in our passage. Where in those four verses does the statement of the condition end and the command begin? If we write a conditional sentence (like the one you are now reading), we are careful to place a comma at the end of the statement of the condition and before the main body of the sentence itself (just as we have done in this sentence). In modern English, it is primarily the punctuation that enables the reader to know which portion of a sentence is the condition. Unfortunately, ancient Hebrew used no punctuation; indeed punctuation is a modern device for which we ought to be most grateful. The translator of the Hebrew text must decide where the conditional clause ends and the body of the sentence begins. He or she may easily spot the beginning of the conditional clause by means of the Hebrew equivalents of our conditional words, such as "if" or "when." But spotting the end of the conditional clause (technically called the "protasis") and the beginning of the main sentence (called the "apodosis") is more difficult. The translator must discern the sense of the sentence and on that basis make a decision regarding where to place the all-important comma in the English translation.

The problem is acute in our passage, 24:1-4. Some translations have proposed that the apodosis of the sentence begins early in the passage—as early as the second half of the first verse. The King James translation is an example. It reads,

> When a man hath taken a wife, and married her, and it come to pass that she find no favour in his eyes, because he hath found some uncleanness in her: *then* let him write her a bill of divorcement, and give it in her hand, and send her out of his house [emphasis added].

Given this translation, the verse is made to read like a law concerning divorce. The husband must divorce his wife with a written statement delivered into her hands, when he has found some uncleanness in her. Contrast this translation with the one we find in the New English Bible:

> When a man has married a wife, but she does not win his favour because he finds something shameful in her, and he writes her a note of divorce, gives it to her and dismisses her; and suppose after leaving his house she goes off to become the wife of another man, and this next husband turns against her and writes her a note of divorce which he gives her and dismisses her, or dies after making her his wife—*then* in that case her first husband who dismissed her is not free to take her back to be his wife again after she has become for him unclean [emphasis added].

The signal word in each translation is "then." In each it has been used by the translators to mark the end of the description of the condition and the beginning of the statement of the regulation. Notice that the King James rendering of the passage begins the apodosis in the second half of the first verse, while the New English Bible does not end the conditional clauses until verse 4. The result of the modern translation is that the verses are no longer a law about divorce, but a law prohibiting the remarriage of a couple who have been divorced and after the wife has married another man.

There seems no doubt among contemporary translators and scholars that the rendering of the passage in the New English Bible is the correct one. (See also the Revised Standard Version. The *Good News Bible: The Bible in Today's English Version* makes the extended conditional statement very clear.) The older translations were an understandable but serious mistake. They were understandable because the conditional statement in this passage is long and involved; it actually goes on for three verses. Hence it is easy to misunderstand where the break between the two parts of the sentence should come. But it was a serious mistake, for it radically transforms the meaning of the passage. The older translations give the impression that this passage is a statement regarding divorce and when it is permissible. But modern scholarship, with a better and more careful study of the Hebrew text, shows that that is not the sense of the passage at all. We must give attention in a moment to the question of whether or not the statements in verse 1 are to be taken as legislation at all, since they appear here as part of the conditional clause. But for now, we must make clear that the primary thrust of the passage has to do with the prohibition against a renovation of a broken marriage. The major commentators on this passage agree with the tendency of modern translators in insisting that it is the renovation of a dissolved marriage that is forbidden here. Suddenly we see this passage in a new light. In a sense, we may say that when understood properly this passage makes it unanimous that the Old Testament does not have a general law regarding divorce. But before we come to that conclusion we must investigate this puzzling passage further.

The passage seems to say (when properly translated) that a divorced woman who has remarried a new husband and is divorced a second time (or widowed) is unclean, so far as her relationship with her first husband is concerned. But why? The reason for such a declaration is obscure, to say the least, if not downright senseless. If the woman has been married to another man and is now freed of her obligation to him, why should she not be allowed to return to the first husband if they both desire it? Commentators who dare to venture a possible reason (beyond simply saying that the reason is "obscure") offer only speculation. Here are a few of the possibilities most often proposed:

1. The prohibition against the renovation of the first marriage might be designed to discourage hasty divorce. A husband knows that when he divorces his wife and she marries another he will never be able to marry her again. That being the case, he is going to consider the act of divorce very carefully before he takes that step.

2. The prohibition might protect second marriages from the ex-husband who now has second thoughts about his divorce; and it also protects against the possibility of the wife threatening to return to her first husband. The incidents in modern society of the jealous ex-spouse trying to interfere in the new marriage are frequent enough for us to see this as a viable reason for the prohibition.

3. The prohibition may assume that the renovation of a dissolved

marriage constitutes adultery. But this seems unlikely since it is not so stated. Moreover, if the woman's second marriage is not considered adulterous, why should remarriage to her first husband be deemed adultery? Still further, the regulation that adultery is punishable by death in Deuteronomy 22 is nowhere alluded to in this passage.

4. Some have understood this prohibition as a simple instance of "taboo." It is based upon a very primitive concept of sexual relationships that reflect cultural practices beyond rational explanation. If such is the case, we have here an example of the "cultural clothing" we mentioned at the beginning of this chapter. We cannot, of course, be critical of such irrational cultural prohibitions, since we know too well that they are not limited to ancient cultures. We can very easily cite such mores in our own culture.

This somewhat strange law against the renewal of a dissolved marriage does not seem to have been widely known in ancient Israel. We can cite two examples from other Old Testament literature where it would seem that the law might have applied; but in each case there is no reference to it. The first is 2 Samuel 3:14-16. David asks that his former wife, Michal, be restored to him, even though she has since been married to another. No mention is made of this being an improper action on the part of David. Nor do we hear any such reservation expressed in Hosea. If we understand the first three chapters of that book correctly, the prophet has divorced his wife, Gomer, for adultery, but in 3:1 he is asked to go and reunite himself with her even though she is loved by another man now. While Deuteronomy and Hosea have a number of features in common, it is interesting that this prohibition against the renovation of a marriage is not mentioned in the prophetic book. As a matter of fact, we might mention here that there is ancient Islamic law that is just the opposite of our passage. It declares that the renovation of a dissolved marriage cannot take place unless there has been an intervening marriage of one of the spouses to another person. (See the article by John Paterson cited above.) Hence, whatever the reason for this law in the book of Deuteronomy might be, we cannot find support for it elsewhere in the Old Testament or the culture of the time.

The reason for the prohibition against the renovation of a first marriage lies beyond discovery, it appears. Far be it from us to venture any conclusion on a matter that stymies even the most learned Old

Testament interpreters. So, having established that the verses have to
do with a prohibition against remarriage of spouses after the woman
has had an intervening marriage, let us probe other issues in the
passage.

We must ask now to what degree verse 1 of our passage suggests
that divorce is mandatory when the condition described there exists.
That is, does verse 1 seem to say that if a husband finds a wife
"shameful" to him, he is *obliged* to divorce her? Or does the verse
suggest only that the husband may be lawfully allowed to divorce her
in such a situation? A related question immediately pops up: what
does the statement "he finds something shameful in her" mean?

It seems clear to us that we must not give the statements in the
conditional part of the sentence the weight of law. That is to say, verse
1 is not a formal institution of divorce. To argue otherwise would be
giving legal status to that which is only intended to describe a situation. The verse only says that if a husband finds something shameful
in his wife and if he then chooses to divorce her, certain consequences
follow. The only safe conclusion is that this verse indicates a tolerance
of divorce. It does not make divorce mandatory; nor does it give
official divine sanction to the practice. What it does in effect is to
recognize that this is a permissible action on the part of the husband.
Hence, the statement of the conditions in this passage makes clear that
divorce was a socially and religiously accepted custom. The right of
divorce was established, apparently, by custom, and there is no knowledge of a law which sanctioned that custom. But our passage forces
us to recognize that divorce was assumed and commonly practiced.
To press the passage to tell us if the practice of divorce was encouraged or only tolerated in Israel is like trying to get philosophy out
of *Sports Illustrated*. From the passage, we simply cannot draw any
more information about the attitude toward divorce than we already
have.

We might add here that the same is true for remarriage after
divorce. Verse 2 indicates that it was permissible for a divorced
woman to remarry. Whether such practice was encouraged or only
tolerated, we cannot say.

But what about this strange statement in verse 1 to the effect that
the husband may divorce his wife if "she does not win his favour
because he finds something shameful in her"? The expression "win his

favour" is a common enough one in the Old Testament (see, for instance, Gen. 6:8; 18:3; 19:19). But what about the reason here for the wife not pleasing her husband—"something shameful in her"? The Hebrew is far more ambiguous than the translation in the New English Bible suggests; and that is unfortunate, for here it appears that we may have some insight into the grounds for divorce as dictated by custom. The Hebrew literally means "the nakedness of a thing." This literal meaning led some of the later rabbis to understand the phrase in this context to mean adultery. But the fact that it is the nakedness of a *thing* combined with the more general expression, "she does not win his favour," led other rabbis to understand the phrase more broadly. They thought that it sanctioned divorce, for instance, if the wife burned her husband's food or if he saw another woman who pleased him better (*Gittin* IX:10 and Josephus, *Antiquities,* IV, viii, 23). The Mishnah took it to mean that the woman broke the law or custom or caused her husband to do so (*Kethuboth* VII:6).

We hesitate to enter such a classical rabbinical difference of interpretation, but we must venture some judgment. It seems unlikely to us that the expression refers to adultery, since Deuteronomy 22:23-27 clearly declares that adultery is to be punished by death. The use of the Hebrew words meaning "something indecent" in 23:14 points in the direction of some behavior that is unbecoming rather than something that is immoral. Perhaps it has to do with some public behavior that causes the husband great embarrassment. It is possible, too, that childlessness was the most common ground for divorce and is the reference of the "shameful" behavior of 24:1. When all is said and done, however, we have only the very vaguest conception of what grounds were regarded as sufficient for divorce. The important point, we think, is that the statement does indicate that some grounds for divorce were required by custom. Divorce could not be simply at the whim of the husband but had to be be rooted in some unbecoming behavior on the part of his wife.

This leads us to further observations concerning the custom of divorce hinted at in this passage. Not only was it necessary for the husband to find something unbecoming in his wife's behavior. It was necessary to put in her hands a bill of divorce. This statement probably shows an advance in Hebraic divorce practices. The divorced woman had a written document which showed that she was formally divorced and hence free to remarry without being charged with adultery. Many believe that in Hosea 2:2 we have a sample of the divorce formula: "She is not my wife and I her husband." (NEB) The bills of divorce became much more elaborate as the years passed, but this simple statement may have been all that was necessary. With this statement delivered to her the wife is sent from the house, and the divorce is finalized. Indeed, to be sent away or to be dismissed is the most common Hebrew expression for divorce (see Deut. 21:14; 22:19, 29; Isa. 50:1; Mal. 2:16). The divorced woman was known as the "expelled" (*gerushah*). Notice that divorce was a family matter. There was no recourse to the courts, no legal formalities. It was a matter strictly between the husband and wife.

But notice, too, that the right of divorce was strictly a male privilege. It was the husband alone who could initiate divorce. To be sure, he had to have some grounds; he had to write the bill of divorce; and he had formally to send his wife away. But it was the husband alone who held the power of divorce in his hands. Perhaps the story of Abram, Sarai, and Hagar in Genesis 16 suggests the arbitrariness of the husband in ancient Israelite culture. Our passage, on the other hand, demonstrates that custom had begun to control the power of the husband and to protect the woman in the marriage relationship. Indeed, later developments in Jewish interpretation of the law moved toward greater and greater protection of the rights of women. The legislative interpretation of the Talmud, however, never goes so far as to allow the woman the right to initiate divorce. But among the Jewish Aramaic writings found in Egypt, and dating from as early as the fifth century before Christ, another segment of Jewish practice has been discovered. Among those writings are a number of marriage contracts which prove that Jewish women in that community did have the right of divorce. (See the work by Reuven Yaron, *Introduction to the Law of the Aramaic Papyri* [Oxford: Clarendon Press, 1961], chapter V.)

It remains for us to look briefly at the concluding sentence of our passage: "This is abominable to the LORD; you must not bring sin upon the land which the LORD your God is giving you as your patrimony." (vs. 4*b*) Our conditional law concludes with one of those motivational clauses mentioned earlier. The writer hopes to stir the reader to obey the law just set forth. Obedience is motivated through the assertion of God's abhorrence of the renovation of a marriage. The sentence presumes the strong sense of Hebraic solidarity, so evident in the Old Testament. If one sins by restoring a marriage in the case described in the law, the whole land sins. Remember we mentioned that the whole of Deuteronomy was characterized by a homiletic style. Our passage exhibits that style with this last exhortation. The law is now transformed from a purely legal, secular-sounding prohibition into a religious injunction. One can almost hear this being read in the context of a worship setting.

It is time for us to summarize what we have found in our examination of Deuteronomy 24:1-4 before we go on to a summary of the Old Testament in general on divorce and remarriage. First, it might be well to summarize exactly what is prescribed in our passage itself. Let us do this by means of a graphic layout of the passage:

THE SITUATION: *If these conditions exist—*

A man marries a woman.

But she does not win his favor because he finds something shameful in her.

And he writes her a note of divorce,

gives it to her and dismisses her.

She then goes off to become the wife of another man.

And this next husband turns against her

and writes her a note of divorce which he gives her and dismisses her;

or he dies after making her his wife.

THE PROHIBITION: *Then this regulation applies—*

Her first husband who dismissed her is not free to take her back to be his wife again

after she has become for him unclean.

THE MOTIVATION: *This regulation is to be obeyed because—*

> This is abominable to the Lord.
>
> You must not bring sin upon the land which the Lord your God is giving you as your patrimony.

Viewing it in this manner, we have been able to conclude a number of things about this passage:

First, it is not legislation concerning divorce and remarriage in general, but rather a prohibition against reestablishing a marriage previously dissolved and after there has been an intervening marriage on the part of the woman.

Second, we were not able to establish a clear reason for this unique regulation. Most likely it was designed either to protect second marriages or else is based upon a simple, irrational taboo.

Third, from the conditions described in verses 1-3 we were able to draw some conclusions concerning the divorce practices of the Hebrews at least by the seventh century: (a) Divorce was practiced, although we see no evidence that it was sanctioned by divine command or encouraged in any explicit way. It was simply allowed and tolerated. (b) Custom dictated that the man alone had the right to initiate a divorce. (c) But he had to have some grounds, most likely some evidence of unbecoming behavior on the part of the woman. (d) The customary divorce procedures included writing a statement of divorce, delivering it into the hands of the woman, and formally dismissing her from the house. (e) The customs of divorce implicit in these verses also reveal that the woman was free to remarry after having been divorced by her husband.

Fourth, from the concluding sentence of the passage, it is clear that this somewhat strange law was given divine sanction through the use of the motivational clause. For whatever reason, the second marriage of the woman made her unclean for a remarriage to her first husband. And to ignore that dimension of uncleanness was regarded as a serious offense to God which had social repercussions for the whole people of Israel.

Summary and Conclusion of the Old Testament Teachings on Divorce and Remarriage

When at last we properly understand Deuteronomy 24:1-4, a

strange fact stares us in the face. The fact is that the Old Testament has no general legislation regarding divorce and remarriage. The practice of divorce is nowhere officially instituted. The right to remarry is nowhere officially granted. This is surprising in the light of the fact that Old Testament legislation so thoroughly covers the situations of life. It is startling, for instance, that the Old Testament lays down regulations concerning diet, but fails either to institute divorce or forbid it. It is little wonder that the rabbis later in their interpretative process of dealing with the Torah had to read Deuteronomy 24:1 as basic and general legislation for divorce. For they knew, as indeed we know, that the religious person must be given some guidance on this crucial issue of breakdown in the marital relationship. If one is to be faithful to God, it is likely that he or she will need to know what faithfulness means in regard to dissolving the bond of marriage.

We urged early in this chapter that the reader understand the Old Testament to be an expression of revelation clothed in cultural practices and mores. Our discussion has highlighted the importance of that understanding when searching the Old Testament for what it has to say about divorce and remarriage. For we find that what we are left with by the conclusion of our search is *legislation which governs custom.* That is, if the revelation of God is found in the divorce and remarriage legislation of the Old Testament, all that it does is offer certain regulations upon the customs and mores of the culture. No Old Testament legislation actually institutes divorce. But such legislation as there is does show one clear and unquestionable direction. It is to attempt to humanize divorce and remarriage practices.

The legislation tries to bring some greater degree of justice into this realm of human behavior. In divorce matters, we have found the tendency toward greater and greater protection of the rights of women. If we were to venture a judgment as to the revelation of God found in this legislation, it would be something like this: God is concerned in situations of divorce and remarriage, as in all situations in which humans find themselves, to protect the dignity of the powerless. If the woman may be regarded as the underdog in ancient Hebraic divorce practices—as indeed we believe she must be—then the legislation of the Torah tends to move toward siding with the underdog. That view is consistent with the totality of the concept of God found in the Old Testament. Always, it seems, we find Yahweh declaring himself in support of justice for the weaker parties. Indeed, the whole story of the Hebrew people finds this point central. God relates himself to a small, powerless band of humans, rescues them from slavery, and works in their history to reveal himself. Hence, we must conclude that, meager though the evidence may be in the Old Testament, the legislation concerning divorce and remarriage is harmonious with the central affirmation of the nature of God revealed to the Hebrew people.

But what can we surmise from the customs of the people? The legislation often informs us more about the customs of the Hebrew people than it does about the will of God. We have found that divorce and remarriage were practiced as a commonly accepted privilege. This is so in spite of the fact that the Hebrews held a very high view of marriage. If we may take Genesis 2:24 as a statement of the Hebraic regard for marriage, it is a noble and divine view. Yet they did not hesitate, apparently, to accept the notion that the spiritual union described in Genesis 2:24 could be dissolved. A separation of the oneness of the married couple was not only allowable but frequent, apparently.

Christians, standing on the other side of the revelation of God in Christ, might demur before this general custom. They may ask whether or not the divorce and remarriage customs of the Hebrew people were harmonious with the process of revelation taking place amid their history. Considering the nature of marriage clearly affirmed in the second creation story, were the Hebrew people wrong to allow divorce and remarriage? Is this custom another garment of the cultural clothing which we Christians should strip away from the Old Testament and discard? That may well be the case, just as we have discarded the practice of polygamy so common especially among the patriarchs of the book of Genesis.

But before we discard that garment, let us consider respectfully its origins. The Hebrew people were a people living constantly in the face of the ever-expanding revelation of God. They were increasingly sensitive to the moral and just nature of the God whom they worshiped. They heard the prophets proclaim God's insistence on social justice in every aspect of human behavior. Yet they never doubted that their custom of allowing divorce and remarriage was fundamentally just. To be sure, they had to work to protect persons more fully against oppressive divorce practices. But that divorce and remarriage were basically justified in the light of their religious faith they never seem to doubt. This may have been due only to another of their blind spots. Perhaps it is the case that they allowed divorce only because they were a "stiff-necked people." Perhaps they failed to see the implications of God's revelation in their midst for this practice.

On the other hand, perhaps they knew that divorce and remarriage were logical necessities given the revelation of their God. It may be that they never fundamentally questioned this practice because it seemed to them a righteous and just possibility. They knew, as we do, the sober fact that marriages become unbearable and destructive of personal dignity. They found in the experience of their years as a people under God that not every marriage is able to progress toward or achieve or sustain the ideal expressed in Genesis 2:24. Hence, as the expression of their rudimentary sense of human justice based upon the revelation of God, they allowed the possibility of divorce and remarriage.

Before we can resolve the question of the defensibility of Hebraic divorce and remarriage customs, we must pursue our study further. What is the thrust of the revelation of God contained in the New Testament regarding divorce and remarriage? We Christians view the Old Testament through the transforming window of the revelation of God in Christ. If we look through that window back into the Old Testament, how is our perception changed? What insights and what failures of the Hebrew people are brought to light when they are examined from the lofty vantage point of the gospel? Our trek through the Old Testament has brought us only to the end of the first leg of our total journey. We have now to begin the second, and perhaps more rewarding, segment of our trip.

2

BUT I SAY UNTO YOU
Divorce and Remarriage in the Gospels

When looking for guidance on any question, the Christian instinctively asks what, if any, kind of direction there might be in the words attributed to Jesus in the four Gospels of our New Testament. Hence, in this chapter we turn our attention away from the Old Testament to the Gospels. While we honor the Old Testament as Scripture, we know that the early Christians believed that Jesus had brought a new and more immediate reign of God in the lives of persons. Therefore, the teachings of the Old Testament always stand under the critical eye of the fuller revelation of God in Jesus of Nazareth. The Old Testament law sometimes stands in a certain tension with the teachings of Jesus. As the Gospel of Matthew puts it so well in what are called the "antitheses" of the Sermon on the Mount (Matt. 5:21-48), "You have learned that our forefathers were told . . . but what I tell you is this." (NEB) The early Christians found that the teachings of the Old Testament paled in importance by the immediate will of God expressed in the Christ figure. Like the stage setting for a play, the Old Testament was an important backdrop for the birth of Christianity. But the focus of the action was not on the setting—not on the background—but front stage in the words and actions of the living actor —in this case, Christ.

What were the teachings of Jesus on the issues of divorce and remarriage? How did he differ from his Hebraic ancestors and their beliefs about God's will for marriage? To ask such a question raises difficulties. We know that the Gospels and their representations of the teachings of Jesus were not concerned simply to give us photographs of what Jesus did and tape recordings of what he said. The four Gospels of our New Testament are rather like impressionistic paintings. They take their original inspiration from the historical facts of the life of Jesus, but they are more concerned to proclaim the good news of what God had done in Christ. They do not want to present strict history—how much duller they would be if that were the case. They desire to address their readers with immediately relevant material for the life of the church. Consequently, they use the stories and sayings they knew that may have originated with the historical Jesus. But they interpret those stories and those sayings so as to make them applicable to the lives of Christians in the time of the writing of the Gospels. Moreover, they write with the conviction that the Christ figure still speaks to the church. It was not that he had once preached on the shores of the Sea of Galilee and now was silenced. If so, all the Gospel writers could do was report what once had been spoken by Jesus. But, no, it was believed Christ continued to speak through the interpretations of the traditional materials and through the minds of the Gospel writers.

The sayings of Jesus in the Gospels about divorce and remarriage, or any matter, therefore may indeed root in the historical figure Jesus. Or they may represent what Christians of the time believed that the living Christ was saying to them. Either way, the Gospel writers believed that they were preserving in writing the words of their Lord. So far as the early Christians were concerned, the sayings recorded in the Gospels represent the will of God for the church at that time.

When we turn to the recorded words of Jesus in the Gospels about divorce, we must be conscious of two settings in which each saying might have originated or been interpreted: The first possible setting is the ministry of the historical Jesus. The second is the struggles of the early Christian community to understand the meaning of Christian discipleship in their day. But this is not our major concern. We will be content to believe that these words represent what the writers of the Gospels believed to be the will of Christ—either through the historical figure of the past or the living, resurrected Lord. So we feel justified in speaking of these as the teachings of Jesus regardless of whether or not the historical Jesus actually spoke just such words.

Our study of the teachings on divorce and remarriage attributed to Jesus in the Gospels will require that we touch on three subjects: First, we will examine the words of Jesus on the Old Testament regulations regarding divorce (Mark 10:2-9 and Matt. 19:3-8). Second, we will look at the saying of Jesus about divorce and remarriage found in various forms in four different places in the Gospels (Matt. 5:31-32 and 19:9; Mark 10:11-12; and Luke 16:18). And third, we will try to understand these passages in the context of Jesus' total message.

Jesus' Words on the Old Testament Regulations regarding Divorce (Mark 10:2-9 and Matthew 19:3-8)

In this short little narrative (in two forms) we find Jesus emphasizing God's intention in creation for the institution of marriage. It is the narrative of a dialogue. Jesus is asked a question to which he responds with another question. When he has heard the response to his question, he states his position on the matter. The whole dialogue takes place in an atmosphere of tension, for Mark and Matthew tell us that those who questioned Jesus did so in hopes of entrapping him (Mark 10:2 and Matthew 19:3). But before our discussion goes any further, read the two passages for yourself in the parallel chart on the facing page.

The story in both Mark and Matthew is typical of what the form critics of the synoptic Gospels have called an "apophthegm" or a "pronouncement story." There are a large number of short narratives about Jesus in discussion with others that conclude with a pithy pronouncement from Jesus. A good example is Mark 2:15-17. In this kind of form there is a short narrative, usually a brief description of some circumstances, followed by a concise dialogue between Jesus and another group (often his opponents). The dialogue will often involve (as it does in the passage we are studying) a question posed by the other group. The dialogue invariably concludes with a word of Jesus that puts to rest the issue under consideration.

This form of narrative and saying may well have originated in the actual ministry of Jesus himself. It is entirely conceivable that in his ministry Jesus had such encounters with opponents who raised objections to his teachings or actions and that in response to them Jesus articulated his view sharply and succinctly. The stories have been preserved in the oral transmission of the words of Jesus in an abbreviated form—the narrative only outlined and the words of the opposing group condensed, as a sort of framework in which to preserve the pronouncement of Jesus. But we can also imagine that the form was relevant for the life of early Christians too. They may have been confronted by opponents in their own day who raised objections

Jesus' Words on the Old Testament Regulations regarding Divorce

Mark 10:2–9 (NEB)	Matthew 19:3–8 (NEB)
2 The question was put to him: "Is it lawful for a man to divorce his wife?" 3 This was to test him. He asked in return, 4 "What did Moses command you?" They answered, "Moses permitted a man to divorce his wife by note of dismissal." 5 Jesus said to them, "It was because your minds were closed that he made this rule for you; 6 but in the beginning, at the creation, God made them male and female.	3 Some Pharisees came and tested him by asking, "Is it lawful for a man to divorce his wife on any and every ground?" 4 He asked in return, "Have you never read that the Creator made them from the beginning male and female?" and he added,
7 For this reason a man shall leave his father and mother, and be made one with his wife; 8 and the two shall become one flesh. It follows that they are no longer two individuals: they 9 are one flesh. What God has joined together, man must not separate."	5 "For this reason a man shall leave his father and mother, and be made one with his wife; 6 and the two shall become one flesh. It follows that they are no longer two individuals: they are one flesh. What God has joined together, man must not separate." 7 "Why then," they objected, "did Moses lay it down that a man might divorce his wife by note of dismissal?" 8 He answered, "It was because your minds were closed that Moses gave you permission to divorce your wives; but it was not like that when all began."

to their beliefs and practices. Their response to such objections might well have been a pithy saying attributed to their Lord. Take for example another pronouncement story, that on the question of paying taxes to Caesar (Matt. 22:15-22; Mark 12:13-17; Luke 20:20-26). We can well imagine that such a question arose in the early church and that a word of the Lord was preserved in the form of a pronouncement story just to resolve it.

That the sayings of Jesus should take on such fixed forms during the period they were remembered and transmitted orally should not surprise us. Narratives and sayings preserved orally rather than in writing tend to take on patterns. Our culture is primarily oriented to the written preservation of material, but one instance of oral preservation we still have is jokes. Hence, jokes very often seem to fall into certain types or forms. Think for instance of ethnic jokes, or jokes about this or that person dying and meeting St. Peter at the gates of heaven. Think of the many joke series, such as the old elephant or the "knock-knock" jokes of some years ago. They invariably followed similar forms. In that way they are more easily remembered. The framework is fixed. All that is changed is the particular content of this joke. In a comparable manner, incidents in the ministry of Jesus and his words were fitted into "frameworks"—one of which is the pronouncement story. In these forms they were transmitted until finally reduced to written expression in our Gospels.

Before us then in the words of Jesus regarding the Old Testament regulations on divorce we have an instance of a pronouncement story. In this case the narrative is nearly nonexistent, and we have only a brief dialogue between Jesus and his questioners. What is important is that the story concludes with the pronouncement of Jesus on the matter of divorce. (See Rudolf Bultmann, *The History of the Synoptic Tradition* [New York: Harper & Row, 1963], and Vincent Taylor, *The Formation of the Gospel Tradition* [London: Macmillan and Co., 1935].)

A reading of the parallel accounts of this dialogue in Mark and Matthew points up a number of differences which we will note but not dwell on: First, it is obvious that there is a different arrangement of the dialogue. The same sayings are in both, but the dialogue proceeds in a slightly different way in the two Gospels. Second, Matthew specifically calls the questioners of Jesus Pharisees (vs. 3). Certain of the ancient manuscripts of the Mark passage also specify that the questioners are Pharisees. Third, you will note that the original inquiry is different. Mark has the question simply: is it lawful to divorce? But Matthew has the question posed in such a way as to focus upon the grounds of divorce: "Is it lawful for a man to divorce his wife *on any and every ground?*" This different focus is also reflected in the concluding word of Jesus in the Matthean form of the story: "I tell you, if a man divorces his wife for any cause other than unchastity, and marries another, he commits adultery." (19:9, NEB) (We have not included this saying in our discussion here because it has to do with the matter of remarriage after divorce. You will find it, therefore, discussed in the next section of this chapter.)

We believe, along with the majority of New Testament scholars, that Mark's story is the older of these two. We think that Matthew has copied Mark at this point and adjusted his account slightly so as to address more directly a concern of the church of his time. Generally, it is thought that Mark's Gospel was the first written (around A.D. 70) and that Matthew and Luke each copied and adapted portions of Mark when they wrote their Gospels (around A.D. 85). In the two accounts we have before us there is a good example of how the later Gospel writers used Mark. Sometimes they quoted him exactly (compare vss. 6-9 in Mark with 4-6 in Matthew). But they adapted the account of the words and ministry of Jesus to their own purposes and needs. In the discussion that follows, we will focus on the account in Mark almost exclusively, since it appears to be closer to the original words of Jesus.

Before looking exclusively at the account in Mark, however, it would be well to ask if there is a conceivable reason for the manner in which Matthew, it seems, has reshaped the story so radically. We have noted that Matthew shifts the entire discussion by changing the initial question posed to Jesus. How could such a shift be explained? Certainly one possibility is that Matthew found it unthinkable that Pharisees would ever ask a question like the one in Mark. Simple verisimilitude would prevent Matthew from allowing the Pharisees to ask, "Is it lawful for a man to divorce his wife?" For he knew that any Jew of the first century, certainly one learned in the Torah, would know that of course it is permissible. That would be like a modern dramatist having the character playing an American politician ask,

"Are presidential elections held every four years in America?" So perhaps Matthew changed the initial question thinking that he was correcting a faulty understanding of Jews as represented in Mark's Gospel.

But another reason Matthew might have had for altering the question directed to Jesus is that he and his community were very interested in the matter of the legitimate grounds for divorce. Our knowledge of first-century Judaism is meager, and we must be careful not to issue generalizations. But there is some evidence that among Jewish rabbis of the time of Jesus a lively debate raged over the question of the grounds for divorce. One group of interpreters, led by Rabbi Hillel, believed that the Old Testament law meant that the husband could divorce his wife if she displeased him for *any* reason. Another group of interpreters, led by Rabbi Shammai, understood it differently. They took the Hebrew words recorded in Deuteronomy 24:1 to mean that the wife must be guilty of some indecency. That indecency, they decided, was marital unfaithfulness; therefore, they permitted divorce only on the grounds of sexual infidelity. (See *Everyman's Talmud,* ed. A. Cohen [New York: E. P. Dutton, 1949].)

It appears that Matthew's church had become involved in the same kind of struggle. The church with which he was affiliated seems to have been composed of a good many Christians who had once been Jews, and perhaps they brought this question about the grounds for divorce from their Judaic background into the church. Matthew, therefore, adapts the words of Jesus (under what he believed to be divine guidance) to address this pressing question in his church. The result is that he has Jesus side with those who saw unfaithfulness as the only legitimate grounds for divorce.

Mark's Gospel, on the other hand, is more likely to have emerged from a setting in the Hellenistic, Gentile world of the first century and was written to a predominantly Gentile congregation. The Jewish interpretations of Old Testament regulations on divorce were probably less well known or at the very least were less readily accepted. This is vividly suggested later in chapter 10 by the fact that Mark has Jesus recognize the possibility of a wife's divorcing her husband (vs. 12). Such a possibility was conceivable in parts of the Greco-Roman world, apparently, but hardly thinkable in Palestinian Judaism. For these reasons, then, Matthew's change in the story appears as understandable and makes it seem likely that Mark's report of the dialogue is the earlier of the two. Therefore, we can focus our attention on the account in Mark. (See Norman Perrin, *The New Testament: An Introduction* [New York: Harcourt Brace Jovanovich, 1974].)

The question posed to Jesus is simply, "Is it lawful for a man to divorce his wife?" But it was an important question. We can imagine it in either the time of Jesus himself or later during the early years of the church when the Gospels were being written. The societies of the Roman Empire in the first century were in the midst of transition. Old practices were everywhere being challenged, much as they are today in America. It was natural, then, that the institutions of society, like marriage, were frequently discussed. Divorce was a subject of disagreement everywhere. So it may be that the religious authorities of the time of Jesus tried to entice him to issue an unpopular view of divorce. Or it may be the early Christians, caught in the throes of social change, who sought from their living Lord some direction regarding the matter of divorce.

To this question about the legality of divorce, Jesus responds with a simple counter-question: what is the teaching of Moses recorded in the books of the law? Perhaps Jesus sensed the motive of the questioner, namely, to entrap him in his own words. So Jesus simply reverses the direction of the conversation to put the interrogator on the defensive and thus take the offensive role himself. On the other hand, the reply Jesus gives is nothing other than a typical rabbinical response: "We must return to Moses and what he commanded with regard to this matter." Jesus is thereby framing the discussion properly from the perspective of the devout Jew. Hence, with this response the discussion shifts in two directions. The inquirers are now asked to participate in a different way and the whole discussion returns to the command of Moses.

The reply to Jesus' question is clearly a summary of the law in Deuteronomy 24:1-4 which we discussed in the previous chapter. Divorce among the Jews of the first century was the peculiar privilege of the male. Jesus' question is answered in a solidly orthodox Jewish manner for that day!

But how unorthodox and startling is Jesus' response to his questioners! It is sometimes said that his response was only a way of putting religious arrogance and smugness in its place. This view contends that Jesus' words here are not intended as a statement on divorce itself, but only as a refutation of those who can so easily answer every question by appeal to a fixed religious authority. And indeed there is some truth in this view. The Jesus represented in the Gospels opposes any kind of neat religious legalism which always has the quick answer. He demands a more thoughtful and committed personal involvement in the quest for the will of God. (See V. Norskov Olsen, *The New Testament Logia on Divorce* [Tübingen: J. C. B. Mohr, 1971], p. 134.)

But we cannot believe that the content of Jesus' answer here is only a statement of opposition to religious legalism. More is given us than that very important point. Jesus replies to the summary of the Old Testament view of divorce with a powerful assertion of the divine intent for the institution of marriage. He does this with a brazen statement of the reason for the Old Testament law on divorce. It is, he asserts, a compromising law, for its only basis is in the inability of humans to fulfill the true intent of God! Moses' law a compromise with human sinfulness! Such a view is typical of Jesus' claim to a new and higher authority than the law of Moses. Jesus then presses the matter back to the origin of marriage in the religious thought of the time. God's purpose in creating the institution of marriage, Jesus reminds his listeners, was that male and female become one—an obvious allusion to Genesis 1:27 and 2:24. Jesus refutes his opponents here by interpreting the Old Testament regulation about divorce with the Old Testament statement about the purpose and nature of marriage. He has refuted the Old Testament with the Old Testament!

Jesus has challenged human tradition with the assertion of the absolute will of God. Jesus puts in contrast the traditions and practices of humans and the desire of God for human life. Again, this is typical of the Jesus we find portrayed in the synoptic Gospels. He again and again dares to claim authority for himself by contrasting the commonly accepted practices of the Jewish heritage with assertions of the absolute will of God. (See, for instance, his act of healing on the sabbath, Mark 3:1-6.)

If we look carefully we can discern further reasons for Jesus' stern rejection of the Old Testament practice of divorce. First, he was concerned with the human values that were being ignored in the practice of divorce in the first century. Men held absolute power in divorce matters. There is evidence that divorces were demanded by Jewish husbands for the most inconsequential reasons. At least some of the Jewish teachers of the first century (the school of Hillel) apparently understood the law of Moses to mean that a husband could divorce his wife if for *any* reason she did not please him. Even for merely oversalting her husband's soup! It was a simple matter, apparently, to divorce one's wife. Simply write the formal bill of divorce, place it in her hands, and send her away.

In contrast to this power of divorce in the hands of the husband, the woman was legally almost powerless. It is true that gradually, in the course of Judaism up to the first century, women came to more and more legal and social status. But there were no provisions for a woman to divorce her husband. It is fair to say that divorce was strictly a male privilege. (The one exception seems to have been Jewish communities in Egypt. See the previous chapter.)

Certainly Jesus perceived a cruel injustice being done to women in the divorce law and practices of his day. Jesus was concerned with a basic human value at stake in the divorce law—the dignity of the woman. He valued the basic human dignity of women, as his ministry clearly suggests. The Gospel of Luke especially demonstrates the role of women as followers of Jesus and his respect for them (e. g., 8:1-3). It is only natural, then, that one of his objections to the divorce regulations of Moses was that they dealt the women of the society a terrible injustice. We suggest that Jesus may have sensed and objected to the whole notion that women should be treated as property in the marriage relationship. He objected to the fact that women could be disposed of as easily as one might sell an ox (or more easily). One does not have to be persuaded that Jesus was a women's liberationist in order to believe that he saw the injustice of the treatment of women in divorce practices. Thus, it would appear, he opposes the divorce law of Moses on the ground, first, that it violates basic human values in its treatment of women.

Let us digress just a bit here to mention another interpretation of Jesus' words about the Mosaic law on divorce. Jesus is quoted as saying, "It was because your minds were closed that he made this rule for you." (Mark 10:5, NEB) Some commentators understand these words differently from the way we proposed above. We suggested that Jesus meant by these words that the law of Moses was a concession to human weakness and failure. Others have proposed that Moses' law was an improvement for women. Before the law came into effect, men could divorce their wives by simply chasing them out of the house! The result was that the dismissed woman had no legal document to prove that her relationship with her husband was ended. She was in effect divorced, but had no legal status as divorced in society. The result was that these women had to continue to live in the eyes of society as married women. They had no right of remarriage, because they had no proof of their divorce. The legislation requiring a note of divorce was a step (a tiny one, to be sure) toward the recognition of the rights of women. Jesus may have had this in mind when he said that the legislation was required because humans (men!) were so closed-minded (or so insensitive to the rights of women). (See Vincent Taylor, *The Gospel According to St. Mark* [London: Macmillan and Co., 1952], p. 418.) While we prefer the interpretation we have given, we do believe that this second interpretation captures another aspect of the attitude of Jesus, namely, his concern for the basic dignity of females. That attitude was part of his concern for the human values involved in the divorce practices of his day.

But he was also concerned with what we might call the spiritual values involved in divorce. He directs attention away from the question of whether divorce is justifiable and focuses instead on God's purposes expressed in creation. God's intention was for husband and wife to become a spiritual unity. Jesus claims it is this divine intent, the original ideal of marriage, that makes marriage a permanent relationship. Whatever one may believe about those circumstances under which a marriage may be dissolved, Jesus here insists that we have in mind the nature of true marriage as an intimate relationship in which two individuals are so united as to become a single entity.

With his concern for the human and spiritual values being violated in the practice of divorce in his day, Jesus gives an unequivocal answer to the question of divorce here. It is "no." Divorce could not be allowed because the practice of divorce at the time ignored the basic human dignity of women and because it ignored the ideal of marriage. The original ideal of marriage is that of an indissoluble relationship.

This passage may very well represent the earliest and most important teaching of Jesus on the subject of marriage and divorce. Its main emphasis is that the divine intent was for marriage to be an inviolable unity. In our quest to understand divorce, Jesus' view leads us back to the purpose and intent of marriage. Yet in this short dialogue between Jesus and his opponents, we are given another glimpse of the view of Jesus. The last verse of this paragraph finds Jesus closing his statement with the injunction, "What God has joined together, man must not separate." With this statement Jesus recognizes human nature and the power of human error to undo the intention of God's work. He recognizes that because of human confusion and failures there is always the possibility of the separation of the divinely intended unity. The prohibition against divorce here is a call to fulfill the divine will and purpose. But there is an acknowledgment of the possibility of failure. With that acknowledgment there comes to mind the other dimension of Jesus' preaching—the divine redemption of human error. His words on divorce here recall the intent of God in his creative work. But the Jesus of the Gospels elsewhere proclaims the intent of God in his redemptive work. We must wait before discussing the relationship between these two—creative *vs.* redemptive work—until we have examined another saying of Jesus on divorce as it appears in three of the Gospels.

Jesus' Sayings about Divorce and Remarriage (Mark 10:11-12; Matthew 5:31-32 and 19:9; and Luke 16:18)

The sayings of Jesus in our Gospels are collections of isolated bits of information. These bits had been preserved in the Christian community by word of mouth until finally the Gospel writers began to collect them and link them together. In Mark 10:5-9 and 10:11-12 we have what were probably two isolated sayings of Jesus independent of one another until the evangelist Mark wrote his Gospel. He quite rightly saw their close relationship and brought them together. He knows the story of Jesus' discussion of divorce with his opponents as a public debate. Jesus was teaching publicly when the question of divorce was put to him. But the other saying of Jesus about the subject was probably known to Mark without any context. It was a simple saying without a setting and with no discussion. So Mark suggests in verse 10 of chapter 10 that when Jesus was alone with his disciples they questioned him further on the subject. Thus Mark has linked together two otherwise independent sayings. This is obvious to us when we compare Mark with the Gospel of Matthew. In his Gospel

Matthew links the dialogue about the Old Testament regulation concerning divorce with a different discussion between Jesus and his disciples (19:10-12). (See *Form Criticism,* ed. F. C. Grant [Chicago: Willett, Clark & Co., 1934].)

The short saying on divorce and remarriage is interesting for a number of reasons. It is a saying found not only in Mark but repeated in Matthew and Luke (many of the sayings of Jesus are). But it is also repeated *twice* by Matthew. This has led some scholars to speculate that this saying was known to the writers of Matthew and Luke through two different sources. It was known to them through Mark, upon whose Gospel both Matthew and Luke depended in preparing their own works; but it may also have been known to them through another source to which they had access but which was unknown to Mark. That source would have been a collection of the sayings of Jesus. (Scholars have called this hypothetical source "Q.") In most cases, when we detect that Matthew and Luke have used this collection of the sayings of Jesus, it is where they report words of Jesus that have no parallel in Mark. (An example would be Matt. 7:24-27 and Luke 6:47-49 to which there is nothing comparable in Mark.) But in the case of this saying of Jesus about divorce, it appears likely that Matthew and Luke found it both in Mark and in the collection of the sayings of Jesus that they possessed. Matthew adapted it in his own way from both of his sources, with the result that it appears twice in his Gospel. Luke, perceiving that the same saying is found both in Mark and the collection of the sayings of Jesus, includes it only once. The importance of this suggestion, if we are correct, is just that in this saying about divorce we are dealing with a purported word of Jesus witnessed to *in both of the earliest written accounts we know of*—Mark and the collection of sayings of Jesus used by Matthew and Luke.

The other fascinating thing about this little saying is the variation we find in the form in which it appears in Matthew. Study the chart containing the words of Jesus on divorce and remarriage in the Gospel found on the next page. You will note that in Mark and Luke the saying is almost identical, but in both of the forms in which it appears in Matthew there is a significant difference. Matthew alone includes what has been called "the exception clause." He repeats the saying that forbids divorce except in one case—that of the wife's unfaithfulness. While Mark and Luke have Jesus saying that divorce and remar-

Jesus' Words on Divorce and Remarriage

Mark 10:11–12 (NEB)	Luke 16:18 (NEB)	Matthew 5:31–32 (NEB)	Matthew 19:9 (NEB)
		31 "They were told, 'A man who divorces his wife must give her a note of dismissal.'	
11 he said to them,		32 But what I tell you is this:	9 "I tell you,
"Whoever divorces his wife	18 "A man who divorces his wife	If a man divorces his wife for any cause other than unchastity he involves her in adultery;	if a man divorces his wife for any cause other than unchastity,
and marries another commits adultery against her:	and marries another commits adultery;		and marries another, he commits adultery."
12 so too, if she divorces her husband and marries another, she commits adultery."			
	and anyone who marries a woman divorced from her husband commits adultery."	and anyone who marries a divorced woman commits adultery."	

riage under any circumstances involve adultery, Matthew has an exception. If the wife has been guilty of sexual unfaithfulness, the husband may divorce her and marry again without committing adultery.

Matthew's "exception clause" has been the topic of much controversy. And it is this little clause in Matthew that has gotten the church involved in the impossible question of determining if there has been unfaithfulness in a marriage that ended in divorce. Our major interest in the question is only whether or not we are able to detect which of the two forms of the saying might be the earlier. That is, is the stricter saying that remarriage after divorce always involves adultery (the form in which it appears in Mark and Luke) the earlier and perhaps the original form? Or is the form in which it appears in Matthew—with the exception clause—the earlier and perhaps original form?

There appear to be two ways of accounting for this difference between Matthew, on the one hand, and Mark and Luke, on the other. First, it is possible that the original form of the saying (perhaps even as it was uttered by Jesus) included the exception clause. Matthew then would best represent the original form of the saying. By scribal error, perhaps, the clause "for any cause other than unchastity" was dropped, and Mark and Luke recorded the saying in its shortened form. This view has been advocated by some scholars (e. g., Manfred R. Lehmann, "Genesis 2:24 as the Basis for Divorce in Halakhah and New Testament," *Zeitschrift für die Alttestamentliche Wissenschaft* 72 [1960]: 266). But the majority of New Testament scholars today opt for a second explanation. They maintain that the earlier form of the saying is represented in Mark and Luke. Matthew's longer form is due to the *addition* of the exception clause. The saying as it originated in either the teachings of Jesus or in the early church under the inspiration of the living Christ was simply that no remarriage after divorce was to be allowed. It was Matthew, then, or the tradition before him, that added to the passage the one case in which remarriage was not an act of adultery.

It is our opinion that the second alternative is the better. It is more likely that Matthew (or his tradition) "softened" the hard saying than that the longer form of the saying was either accidentally or intentionally made hard. We are convinced of this for a number of reasons: First, this is the consensus of scholarship on the question. To be sure, consensus does not equal truth! But in the face of such difficult questions we need to be guided by the majority of scholarship.

However, we are convinced of this explanation for another kind of reason. It makes sense that a word of Jesus which is very demanding should tend toward being reinterpreted and made easier. On many occasions in the present-day life of the church such a tendency prevails. It is only human nature that we seek to ease the demands placed upon us. With just a little human sympathy we can imagine the way this happened in Matthew's church. It seemed unfair that a man married to a woman guilty of blatant sexual unfaithfulness should remain married; and that if he did divorce her, he should be forbidden to remarry under threat oi adultery. In the name of basic justice it seems that the drastic demand of the saying on divorce and remarriage should be interpreted in such a way as to allow for exceptions. Out of a process of thought perhaps similar to this the form of the saying recorded in Matthew emerged. Interpretation has tempered demand with justice. Understanding Matthew's form of the saying in this way corresponds to a basic guideline in the critical study of the Gospels. That guideline is that generally the "harder" saying is closer to the original than the "softer" one.

Finally, we think Matthew deliberately adapted the dialogue he found in Mark so as to make it focus on the legitimate *grounds* for divorce. We saw that he altered the initial question posed to Jesus to make it read, "Is it lawful for a man to divorce his wife on any and every ground?" (19:3, NEB) And to conclude the dialogue he had Jesus utter the words we find in Matthew 19:9. Most likely, then, Matthew has adjusted the earlier form of the saying of Jesus as he found it in Mark.

We turn now to a closer comparison of the sayings found in the three Gospels. If the reader examines the parallel of the sayings found in this section, a number of things will emerge:

1. It is said that if a man divorces a woman (except for unchastity), the woman is guilty of adultery. This assertion is unique to Matthew's saying (5:32).
2. If a man divorces his wife and marries again, he is guilty of adultery. This point is made in all three of the Gospels (Mark 10:11; Matt. 19:9; Luke 16:18).

3. If a man marries a divorced woman, adultery is committed. This is found in Matthew (5:32) and Luke (16:18).
4. If a woman divorces her husband and remarries, she is guilty of adultery. This is found only in Mark (10:12).

It would appear that the second point is the original tradition which Mark reported and which in various forms has been repeated by Matthew and Luke. The third point (that if a man marries a divorced woman, adultery is committed) seems to be the result of Matthew and Luke's rewording of Mark's second clause. What Mark has is that if a woman divorces a man and remarries, she is guilty of adultery. But Matthew and Luke, apparently, cannot understand that a woman would divorce her husband (indeed, an unlikely event in those days since it would violate Jewish law). So they have expressed it in terms of the adultery resulting from a man marrying a divorced woman. Very likely their collection of the sayings of Jesus (called "Q") included such a saying. But the effect is that Mark alone among the three Gospels represents the possibility that a woman might divorce her husband.

But what is more important is the fact that among the Gospel writers only Matthew has Jesus saying that *divorce* itself is adultery (except in the case of the charge of unfaithfulness). While Mark and Luke (and Matthew elsewhere) have Jesus saying that it is *remarriage after divorce* that is adulterous, Matthew claims that *divorce* is the offensive act. We can only speculate why this saying in Matthew should appear. Perhaps, in Matthew's logic, divorce was tantamount to adultery because of Jesus' very strict prohibition against divorce (Mark 10:5-9). This logic is perhaps part of Matthew's exception clause. Given Jesus' abhorrence of it, Matthew sees divorce itself as adulterous; but he cannot bring himself to forbid it in cases of unchastity, perhaps because that would imply a prior adultery. Hence he inserts the exception.

Out of this maze of ever so slight, but important, differences among the reporting of the three Gospels one point should stand out. The basic affirmation of the Gospels here is that remarriage after divorce is adultery. What the words of Jesus suggest is that divorce does not dissolve the permanence of marriage. Hence, to remarry after a divorce is adultery, just as it would be adultery to engage in extramarital sexual relations. The primary point seems not to be the adulterous character of divorce, but the actual inability of divorce to dissolve marriage. Adultery results from remarriage after divorce because divorce does not automatically separate the couple bound together in marriage.

What we have found may be summarized briefly in two points: First, Jesus is represented in the Gospels as teaching that divorce is forbidden because it violates God's intention that marriage be the permanent union of two individuals. Second, remarriage after divorce is adultery, for divorce does not dissolve the union of marriage. But we must add to these two main points an additional finding of our study thus far:

We saw that Jesus openly recognized that humans have the potential for thwarting God's intention for marriage. With the simple words, "What God has joined together, man must not separate" (Mark 10:9, NEB), Jesus acknowledges that humans can and do separate what God has united. The absolute will of God is sometimes frustrated by human error and human failure. Behind this simple recognition resides a basic theme of Biblical thought. God's plan for creation has been distorted by human action. Not only the institution of marriage, but the whole of God's created order has been disfigured and warped by human sin (Gen. 3). Jesus recognizes the power of human sin to affect the divine order of things.

The Gospels' Teachings on Divorce and Remarriage in the Context of Jesus' General Message

We must begin to probe beneath the surface of these words to their meaning. Interpretation involves going beyond the literal meaning of the words to their inner sense. Somewhat as a good therapist listens to a client on two levels, we should listen to the Scriptures on two levels. The therapist hears the actual words spoken and grasps their meaning, but she or he is also sensitive to the deeper meaning the words may convey: their emotional content, their function as revelations of the personality of the speaker, and their interrelationship with other aspects of the client's behavior. Interpreters of Scripture have no less a task. They must discern the immediate, evident meaning of the words recorded, but must go on to ask what further meaning these may have for the modern reader in the light of other words and the spirit of the writer-speaker.

It is necessary for us to place the words of Jesus concerning divorce and remarriage in the broader context of his message. As the therapist tries to understand specific words of the client in the framework of the client's total behavior, so we should try to grasp the meaning of Jesus' specific words in the context of his general message. In this way, we hope to discover the inner meaning of the words attributed to Jesus.

Modern interpreters of the Gospels agree for the most part that the central focus of the ministry of Jesus was the proclamation of the kingdom of God (see especially the introduction of Jesus' ministry in Mark 1:14-15). In each of the synoptic Gospels Jesus is represented as declaring that the new and long-awaited reign of God had begun. The concept of the kingdom (or reign) of God is rooted far back in the history of Jewish thought and developed especially in the period *ca.* 500 B.C.—A.D. 70. It was the hope of the Jewish people that God would reassert his reign over creation and drive out all of those forces that were alien to the created order. It was believed that nature and human life were no longer under the reign of God but subject to the forces of evil. Jesus' message was that the reign of evil had come to an end and that the reign of God was becoming reality once again. In the synoptic Gospels Jesus proclaims the advent of the kingdom of God in various ways. The kingdom is repeatedly the subject of his parables (e. g., Matt. 25:1). His wondrous acts of healing and especially his exorcisms seem intended to demonstrate that the forces of evil have had their day and are now overcome by the immediate power of God (Luke 10:18; 11:20). The new authority Jesus claims for himself seems to be premised on the fact that the reign of God is now re-instituted; hence, for instance, he can forgive sin (Luke 5:17-26). He teaches his disciples to pray for the coming of the kingdom (Matt. 6:10; Luke 11:2). In each of the synoptic Gospels the total ministry of Jesus seems centered on the fact of the inauguration of the new reign of God. (Matthew uses the expression kingdom of *heaven* instead of kingdom of God, as found in Mark and Luke, but seems to mean the same reality.) (See Rudolf Bultmann, *Jesus and the Word* [New York: Charles Scribner's Sons, 1935], chapter II.)

The so-called ethical teachings of Jesus are likewise founded upon the concept of the kingdom of God. The precise relationship between Jesus' ethics and his proclamation of the kingdom has been the subject of much debate. (See Richard Hiers, *Jesus and Ethics* [Philadelphia: The Westminster Press, 1968].) But it seems that Jesus intended to describe in his ethical teachings what it means for the reign of God to be complete in human life. To realize the full sovereignty of God in your life, for instance, means not to love just your neighbors but to love even your enemies (Matt. 5:43-44). Obedience to the will of God, apparent everywhere in the teachings of Jesus, is the quality of life under God's rule. We do not think that these teachings are merely descriptions of the utopian world to come in the future; nor are they simply an ethic for the interim period between this age and the kingdom that is to come. Rather, they are examples of how we may actualize the sovereign will of God in our own time. They are, therefore, "kingdom ethics" but of a kingdom whose reality is present and realizable.

The divorce and remarriage sayings of Jesus stand in the synoptic Gospels as part of that view of what it means to live under the reign of God. Here as elsewhere Jesus is describing what life in the kingdom is like. To live under the reign of God is to find in marriage the fulfillment of that union mentioned in Genesis 2. And if that union is fulfilled, divorce will be out of the question; thus to live under God's rule means to avoid divorce by finding in marriage an indissoluble oneness. It is important for us to see that the divorce and remarriage teachings of the Gospels are part of that broader picture painted by Jesus in his ministry. It is a picture of the kingdom of God being realized in the midst of this world. As such it is the realignment of human life with the desire of God. In a word, if we are to actualize the reign of God in our lives, divorce and remarriage will not occur, but marriage will be the unity of a woman and a man as God intended it.

But there is another aspect of the proclamation of the kingdom of God which is related to our specific concern. Jesus announced that the will of God for creation was being reasserted, and he repeatedly insisted that the will of God must not be confused with human custom and tradition. He often draws a sharp distinction between divine will and human practice. The Jewish tradition of fasting, for instance, was not to control the divine will for Jesus and his disciples (Mark 2:18-22; Matt. 9:14-17; Luke 5:33-39). It is not that Jesus denigrated the legal social traditions of his day. He is not saying, "Ignore the traditional practices of society to follow God's will." Jesus' concern was not to destroy the semblance of order that social traditions provide, but to help us see that the divine will goes beyond those social traditions. The divine will is not identical with the social restraints against murder, but permeates the inner being of humans and applies to urges and attitudes as well as overt actions (Matt. 5:21-22). Jesus, in his prophetic character, everywhere decries the simple equating of human customs and divine will. Even his response to the Old Testament law regarding divorce is a warning not to confuse human law with divine will.

Jesus' teachings on our subject then are part of his insistence that social customs not be taken simply as expressions of God's will. His teaching on divorce is part of his protest against a smugness that too easily equates human practices with divine will. Jesus was saying that the kingdom of God meant some radical transformations of human practices and among them the practice of marriage. It is not to be so easily dissolved simply because Moses seems to have allowed it. The coming of the kingdom means that the divine intention of God for marriage is reasserted in the face of common social custom.

When we examine the proclamation of Jesus, it appears that it contains two points of focus. We can perhaps think of them this way:

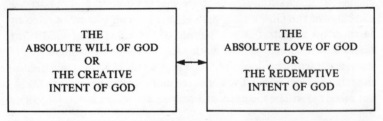

THE
ABSOLUTE WILL OF GOD
OR
THE CREATIVE
INTENT OF GOD

THE
ABSOLUTE LOVE OF GOD
OR
THE REDEMPTIVE
INTENT OF GOD

As we read through the Gospels, we find the sayings of Jesus falling into these two camps. On the one hand, we hear of the demands of God upon those who would live under his reign. We are told, for instance, that nursing anger is the equivalent of murder (Matt. 5:22, NEB) and that lust is the equivalent of adultery (Matt. 5:28). We must hate our parents and even ourselves, if we are to be disciples of Jesus (Luke 14:26). Those who would be disciples must leave the dead unburied (even one's own deceased father) in order to be faithful to their Lord (Luke 9:59-60). Epitomizing this aspect of the teachings of the Jesus of the Gospels is the word in Matthew 5:48: "You must therefore be all goodness, just as your heavenly Father is all good."

On the other hand, we read in the Gospels of God's gracious acceptance and love. The prodigal son is accepted back into the family and fully pardoned of his foolishness (Luke 15:11-32). The lost sheep is sought and found (Luke 15:1-10). The one who is reconciled to God is not the one who is sinless but the one who acknowledges her or his sin and seeks forgiveness (Luke 18:9-14). We see Jesus in constant association with the "sinners" of his day, but we do not hear him condemning them (Mark 2:15-17). Rather, by his association with them he incarnates God's acceptance and love of humanity. What better summary of this aspect of the teachings of Jesus than the word spoken on the cross which pleads that God forgive even his executioners (Luke 23:34)?

What we have is the pronouncement of the *radical demands of God,* on the one hand, and the *radical acceptance of God,* on the other. The full will of God is painted vividly—this is what God desires of humanity. But along with that vivid portrait of the will of God is an equally brilliant presentation of the unending, limitless love of God. The Christian must never read the Gospels blind to one or the other of these two aspects of their teachings. To take seriously only the radical demands of God stated in the Gospels and disregard the radical acceptance of God would cut out the heart of Christianity. But neither will it do to ignore the demands of God and speak only of God's limitless forgiveness and love. Like a favorite dish that has two main ingredients, we cannot have Christianity without both of these aspects of the teachings of Jesus.

Jesus taught that God has a clear and absolute intention for the character and quality of human life. But he is a God who offers unconditional love and acceptance to all, regardless of the degree to which they have managed to conform to that divine will. It is in the context of the divine love and acceptance that Christians are asked to work to make their lives conform to the plan God has for human life. But failure to conform to that will cannot put one outside of the realm of God's love! It is comparable to parents who have ideals and intentions for their children. But the good parents love their children without regard to the extent those children fulfill the parents' ideals.

When we consider the Gospels' teaching on divorce and remar-

riage in the light of this analysis of the teaching of Jesus, things begin
to grow clear. The words of Jesus regarding divorce and remarriage
are part of that aspect of his teachings which stresses the divine
intention for humanity. They are part of the radical demand of God.
But, unlike other parts of the teachings of Jesus that are similarly part
of that radical demand, we have tended in our churches to make law
out of the words about divorce and remarriage. We have tended to
legislate against divorce and remarriage in our denominational bodies.
But it is strange that we have not done the same with other aspects
of Jesus' teachings. We do not insist that persons who confess that
they love their parents be excluded from membership in the church
(Luke 14:26)! If there are some who confess they have had momentary
lustful thoughts about a movie star, we do not insist that they have
their eyes plucked out in accord with the word of Jesus (Matt.
5:28-29). Indeed we do not, for it would be ridiculous to do so! For
these are words of Jesus which express the desire of God that
humanity be sinless and conform to his plan for creation. And we
recognize, too, that they involve a certain degree of overstatement—
exaggeration, if you will. Surely God does not intend us actually to
pluck out our eyes if those organs have been the occasion for our
sinning.

Moreover, these radical assertions of God's creative intention for
humanity found in the teachings of Jesus were never meant to be law
for the Christian. Jesus' whole ministry involved an attack upon a
legalism which attempted to put God's will into precise prescriptions.
His opposition to the religious leaders of first-century Judaism came
precisely at this point. He opposed the use of the Mosaic law as a strict
legislation for religious life. The reign of God that Jesus announced
could not be packaged in the way the Jewish tradition of his day had
attempted to do. We need only recall his teaching on the sabbath
regulation (Mark 2:23-28) and ritual cleansing (Mark 7:14-23). Many
of his radical statements about the will of God were intended to
demonstrate the inadequacies of the legalistic understanding of the
books of Moses in the Old Testament (e. g., Matt. 5). We cannot then,
in faithfulness to Jesus, make of his teachings a new legalism. That
would be like the leaders of a rebellion overthrowing the tyranny of
a nation's officials only to establish a new tyranny once they had
gained power. While the teachings of Jesus vividly present the will of

God for humanity, they are not a new law. To understand them that way does violence to the spirit of the prophet of Nazareth.

We must now view the words about divorce and remarriage in a similar light.The prohibition against divorce and the declaration that remarriage after divorce is adultery are part of Jesus' portrayal of the will of God for his creation. They are not intended to be enforced as legislation any more than some other of the words of Jesus are. We must be all goodness, just as God is all good. That is the goal of our human lives. That is what God intends for us. We must not divorce and then remarry. That is the goal of marriage—that it be indissoluble. That is what God intends for the institution of marriage. But in both cases—the injunction to be all goodness and the injunction that forbids divorce and remarriage—the intent of God, not practical law, is being expressed.

What the general teachings of Jesus do suggest, then, are two things: First, that we understand marriage as God intended it—a permanent union of a man and woman. But, second, that we understand that if human error thwarts God's intention for a marriage, there is forgiveness and divine acceptance available. Just as that divine forgiveness is readily available when we fail to live up to the will of God in other matters! When we are angry, we do not think simply that we are guilty of murder in God's sight. We think rather that God understands our failure and offers us his forgiveness. With that forgiveness comes the opportunity for a new beginning—another chance. So, with divorce, we must acknowledge that the failure to fulfill God's intention for humankind has again occurred. But God is there ready to offer his forgiveness and love to absolve that human sin. With the divine forgiveness comes a new beginning, a new opportunity. In the case of the failure of marriage, that new beginning which comes with God's love sometimes means the opportunity to remarry. God's love offers the opportunity to try again to create a union that is in harmony with his will.

Summary

Our effort to understand the divorce and remarriage passages in the synoptic Gospels has touched on two interrelated points. First, we observed how these passages are part of Jesus' general proclamation of the advent of the kingdom of God. As such they are part of Jesus' description of what it means to live under the immediate reign of God. They form another instance of how Jesus declared that the will of God in the kingdom cannot be equated with human customs and practices. Second, we suggested that Jesus' preaching asserts not only God's radical demands but also his radical acceptance. We found that we could not justify a legalistic adherence to these words which are part of Jesus' portrayal of the intention of God for humanity. Not only are these words *not* intended as law for the Christian; they are to be viewed always in the light of Jesus' proclamation of the redemptive will of God. If the will of God expressed in the prohibition against divorce and remarriage is frustrated, there is still the assurance of God's unfailing forgiveness. The kingdom of God is the reign of love and forgiveness as well as of his absolute will.

The words of Jesus on divorce and remarriage present us with a profound expression of the divine plan for marriage. But they were not meant to be legalistically enforced. They broaden our minds and spirits beyond a simple assertion of "don'ts." They open us to the whole rich message of God's revelation in Christ—the revelation of the meaning of God's reign in creation and of God's loving nature. They open us to the profound and complex nature of marriage and its spiritual dimensions. What all this means for the ministry of the church to divorced and perhaps remarried persons in our society we must weave into whole cloth in the conclusion of our study, after we have completed our survey of the rest of the Biblical material.

We move on then to the apostle Paul and the question of what he had to say regarding our topic. If we may entice you just a bit, let us suggest now that what we will find in the writings of Paul is amazingly harmonious with what we found in the Gospels. That harmony, we believe, adds further credence to the interpretation we have given to the synoptic sayings.

3

THE LORD'S RULING
Divorce and Remarriage in the Apostle Paul

Surely the Christian movement originated in the message of Jesus of Nazareth. But the great literary articulator of early Christian thought seems to have been the apostle Paul. It appears that his epistles were collected at a relatively early date (perhaps by A.D. 90) and were the first of our present New Testament literature to be given something like canonical status. Paul's influence is evident from the number of books in the New Testament attributed to his hand. While we must always beware of overstating the case for the prominence of Paul in the early church, it appears likely from what we know of the literary productions of the early Christians that he occupied a place of indisputable importance. It is safe, therefore, to conclude that next to the figure of Jesus himself, no other person was so influential in shaping early Christianity as was the apostle Paul.

Paul's significance for New Testament investigations is enhanced by another fact. His epistles represent the earliest written material preserved by the Christian community. Whereas students of the New Testament generally regard the Gospels and all the other New Testament writings as originating after A.D. 70, Paul's letters stand on the other side of that landmark date. Ranging from as early as 47 or 50 and proceeding to 56 or 58, his works give us our clearest window into the deepest recesses of the early church. To be sure, we can reconstruct the hypothetical early collection of the sayings of Jesus and argue for the shape and content of the oral tradition incorporated into segments of the Gospels. But we stand on less sandy ground when we look to the epistles of Paul for our knowledge of earliest Christian thought and practice.

It is vital, then, that we ask what the apostle taught concerning the matters of divorce and remarriage. That teaching informs us not only of what Paul himself thought, but of what position was most influential in forming early Christian attitudes toward these important issues. As we will see, Paul's discussion of divorce provides us with the earliest written claim for what Jesus taught concerning divorce and the earliest Christian interpretation and application of that teaching to a concrete situation. Paul's writing on this theme must be comparable to that proverbial link in the chain that ties together earlier segments with later ones; but fortunately in this case it is not a "missing link."

To examine Paul's discussion of divorce and remarriage, we must keep in mind the general nature of his writings and his ministry. Paul was neither a systematic theologian nor a systematic expositor of Christian ethics. He was above all else a practical missionary. His concern was to spread the Christian gospel and to nurture the Christian communities in the Hellenistic world. He articulates important theological positions perhaps for the first time in literary expression. In this sense he can be called the first Christian theologian. But there is danger in such an assessment of Paul, for his purpose was far from that of a church theologian. As a missionary he wrote out of practical concerns. That meant that sometimes he was interested in clarifying belief. The supreme example of that kind of interest is the epistle to the Romans. At other times his concern was with much less theoretical matters, e. g., the collection for the Jerusalem Christians discussed in 2 Corinthians 8 and 9. At still other times his attention was focused on ethical matters such as humility (see for instance Phil. 2). Very mundane and administrative matters confronted him, and he wrote to urge certain courses of action (e. g., Philemon). Often his teaching arises out of a concrete need of the persons he is addressing. He writes to the Thessalonians about the impending parousia (the return of Christ) out of his concern to help them deal with their suffering. Perhaps no letter better represents the mind of Paul as a practical theologian than the epistle to the Galatians. There Paul articulates in writing for the first time (to our knowledge) his insistence that the gospel is a message of justification by faith and not by works of the law. But he does so, apparently, because a confusion has arisen in the churches of Galatia; and Paul desires to correct them. In the epistle to the Galatians one can see how theological reflection results from the concern of the pastor for a community of new Christians struggling to understand their faith. Paul is studied often in the context of Christian doctrine, as the first proponent of central themes in the Christian faith. But perhaps where we ought to place Paul more often than we do is in the context of practical theology. When we are asking the question, "How should Christian faith shape behavior and practice in a concrete situation?", perhaps we should turn to Paul more often than we do.

Hence it is as "practical theologian" and pastor that the apostle Paul addresses himself to the question of divorce. But unfortunately this question did not press upon Paul on many occasions. There are possibly three passages in his epistles in which he speaks to our issue. The most important and central for our study is 1 Corinthians 7:10-16. But divorce is also mentioned by implication in his epistle to the Romans and in 1 Timothy and Titus.

Romans 7:2-3 finds Paul speaking of the obligation of a married woman to her husband:

> a married woman is by law bound to her husband while he lives; but if her husband dies, she is discharged from the obligations of the marriage-law. If, therefore, in her husband's lifetime she consorts with another man, she will incur the charge of adultery; but if her husband dies she is free of the law, and she does not commit adultery by consorting with another man. [NEB]

By implication Paul suggests that marriage is a lifetime obligation. He recognizes that death may free the married woman from that obligation, but his silence regarding divorce suggests that it is not a means by which such an obligation is terminated. But it is unfair of us to employ this passage as a means of probing Paul's attitude toward divorce! The allusion to marriage and its obligation here is used by the apostle as an illustration to make another point. You will note, if you read the context in which this mention of marriage is found, that Paul is discussing the freedom of the Christian from the law (i. e., the law of Moses and law in general as employed as a means of acquiring a right relationship with God). The New English Bible makes this clear by introducing verse 2 with the phrase "For example." By means of this illustration Paul hopes to drive home the point that the Christian is freed from obligation to the law in a manner comparable to the freedom of the widow from the obligations of marriage. From this metaphor we do not know where Paul himself stands on the issue of divorce. The illustration cites common practice among his readers. The only thing we can quite accurately infer is that the people to whom Paul is speaking understood a woman's legal obligation to her husband, and Paul uses that understanding metaphorically. To infer more would be unjust to Paul. The preacher uses an illustration to make a point. The congregation is unfair to the preacher if they attempt to draw more than the one point from the illustration. So let us not press Paul's use of this metaphor any further than we have. Consequently, we can place Romans 7:2-3 to one side as not relevant for the purposes of our inquiry.

The epistles of 1 Timothy and Titus, which bear the name of Paul, refer to faithfulness in marriage as a prerequisite for bishops, deacons, and elders in the church. In the descriptions of the qualities these persons should have, the phrase "faithful to his one wife" is used in each (1 Tim. 3:2, 12; Titus 1:6, NEB). Again, these passages must be disqualified from consideration in our study. First, the passages are too vague to be of use to us. Obviously, the phrase suggests that these leaders in the church should not be guilty of adultery. But that the phrase prohibits divorce is not at all clear. Too many assumptions and outright guesses would be required to infer from this anything about the writer's attitude toward divorce and remarriage. Second, it is widely held that 1 and 2 Timothy and Titus (the pastoral epistles) are not from the hand of the apostle Paul at all. They were more likely written by a faithful follower of the apostle who desired to honor him by attributing these letters to him. By linguistic, stylistic, and theological analyses, these writings are found to be so radically different from the genuine epistles of Paul that we must assign them to another and later author.

We are left with but one gem to place under our magnifying glass for close examination—1 Corinthians 7:10-16. What follows will be an attempt to study this passage for what it tells us of Paul's attitude toward divorce and remarriage. We will follow that by placing the results upon which we can agree within the broader context of Paul's message.

Finally, we will ask what conclusions may be reached regarding Paul's words on divorce in the context of his primary concerns and see how those conclusions relate to what we found in the previous chapter on the Gospels.

hope that reading the verses printed in this pattern helps you
amber of points that must be discussed. The first of these is the
in verse 10: "which is not mine but the Lord's." Contrast that
e 8 in which Paul says simply, "I say this . . ." and verse 12
Paul more explicitly writes, "as my own word, not as the
." What stands out is the fact that Paul claims that the words
resses to the married couples about divorce and remarriage are
ply his own opinion on the matter, but the teaching of none
an Christ himself. Paul often invokes authority for his words.
he writes as he does in the paragraphs to the unmarried and
arried to non-Christian spouses, he invokes the authority of
apostleship. At times he throws the weight of the law of
ehind his exhortations (e. g., 1 Cor. 9:8-9). On the issue of the
women to cover their heads in church he uses tradition or
to uphold his beliefs (1 Cor. 11:2-16). Sometimes, it would
e calls up the arguments of secular writings in support of his
. g., Gal. 5:19-21; Phil. 4:8; see Victor Paul Furnish, *Theology*
hics in Paul [Nashville: Abingdon Press, 1968], pp. 69-72.)
here the appeal is to the "Lord." Paul elsewhere makes use
same appeal to the word of the Lord (1 Cor. 9:14; 11:23;
. 4:15). The question must be asked what Paul means here by
the authority of the word of the Lord. Several possibilities
themselves. The *first* is the most obvious, especially in the case
10 of our passage, namely, that Paul knows of a saying of
out divorce and remarriage similar to those recorded in the
c Gospels. 1 Thessalonians 4:15 and 1 Corinthians 11:23 both
hings for which one could argue that Paul knew words of Jesus
able to sayings preserved in the synoptic Gospels. But in none
cases does Paul offer anything like a quotation of Jesus.
re, (*second*) some interpreters have proposed that Paul does
n to refer to the teachings of the historical Jesus but to the
ion of the living Christ. Does the title "Lord" suggest that
derstands his authority to come from his relationship with the
ted Christ in the community of faith?
ird possibility is a mediating position between these two. It
argued that Paul is appealing to a dynamic tradition in the
That tradition took its origin in the words and ministry of the
al Jesus but was constantly expanded and enriched by those

Paul's Teaching in 1 Corinthians 7:10-16

The fine art of interpretation requires the discipline of seeing a
passage within its larger context. It is much like appreciating one part
of a painting in the light of the total canvas or one movement of a
symphony in the light of the others. To abstract one part from the
whole is to strip away the meaning the originator had for it. How true
this is of Biblical interpretation! To read and attempt to understand
a few verses ripped out of the page is like trying to ride a bicycle wheel
that has been removed from the bike! It is to miss the whole meaning
that was intended in the creation of the passage.

It is necessary, therefore, to construct the setting for verses 10-16
of chapter 7 of 1 Corinthians. First, a few words must be said about
the epistle as a whole. 1 Corinthians is one part of a much larger
correspondence Paul appears to have had with the Christians at Corinth. Scholars suggest that, given the two epistles we have in the New
Testament addressed to the Corinthians and from hints in these of still
other correspondence (1 Cor. 5:9; 2 Cor. 2:3-4, 9; 7:8-12), we can
suppose a series of letters and responses. Over a period of time around
52-54 Paul wrote perhaps four letters to the Corinthians and by letter
and oral report received a number of responses. 1 Corinthians is
probably the first of Paul's letters to that congregation. It appears to
have been written in response to both oral and written messages about
and from the Corinthian Christians. Paul mentions (1:11) that he has
received information about conditions in the Corinthian church from
"Chloe's people" (perhaps relatives or slaves of Chloe) and from some
messengers as well (16:17). Many of the issues he discusses, especially
in chapters 1 through 6, seem to be based on these oral reports he has
received. But in 7:1 the apostle shifts to a consideration of matters
about which the Corinthians have written him. That letter from the
Christians at Corinth to Paul can be reconstructed in part from a
study of the issues with which he deals in chapters 7 through 16. Our
passage stands within the early section of the epistle that appears to
be Paul's response to the letter from the Corinthians. (See Calvin
Roetzel, *The Letters of Paul* [Atlanta, Ga.: John Knox Press, 1975],
pp. 41-51.)

1 Corinthians is a "problem-centered" letter. That is, the entire
letter focuses on those problems that, Paul has learned, exist in the
Christian community at Corinth. He deals with each problem in

order, trying as best he can to help the readers correct their situation. There are some general themes, however, that Paul keeps emphasizing as he proceeds with his pastoral advice. An example is his insistence on the Christian's freedom from worldy standards (e. g., 1:18-24) which again and again reappears in his discussion of specific issues. It can be seen then that the letter is not a carelessly arranged treatment of the problems the Corinthians are having. Paul wants to treat those various problems in the context of what it means for Christians to live in this world as a community of the last days (an eschatological community). Hence, it is not without point that chapter 15 concludes the body of the letter with a discussion anticipating the final days of human history. (See Hans Conzelmann, *1 Corinthians* [Philadelphia: Fortress Press, 1975].)

Within this problem-centered correspondence stands chapter 7. The chapter in general deals with the broad question of the relationship of the sexes in the light of Christian convictions regarding the final days. We would do well to trace the outline of the entire chapter before focusing on the verses that particularly interest us. A general introduction raises the issue of the relation of male and female, states the important role of marriage, but then exhorts Paul's preference for celibacy as a way of life (vss. 2-7). There follows advice to three distinct groups of people in the light of the introduction. First comes the general question, may marriages be contracted among the single persons of the community (vss. 8-9)? Second, married persons are addressed with attention to the question, may marriages be dissolved (vss. 10-11)? Finally, Paul speaks to those persons married to unbelievers. The concerns in these verses (12-16) seem to be two: May they remain married? May they divorce?

In verses 17-24 Paul articulates a general principle that controls much of his thought throughout this section: the Christian should remain in the condition in which she or he was when called by God to embrace the faith. The circumcised should remain circumcised; the slave, a slave; (and later he adds) the married, married; the divorced, unmarried. Paul had anticipated this principle in his discussion in verses 8 and 9.

The next subdivision of this chapter seems to be verses 25-35 in which he argues for his own preference for a celibate state. He suggests at least four reasons why celibacy is desirable for the Christian:

the principle cited in the section above (vs. 2(pains experienced by single persons as compare((vs. 28); the impending parousia (vss. 29-31); an to the Lord possible for single persons (32-3 chapter offers some advice to two additional those related to one another as "partners in celi together but pledged to abstain from sexual rel He defends the right of widows to remarry v care to, but again counsels that the better way 39-40).

It is a temptation to explore the meaning Paul says in this chapter quite apart from hi: remarriage (e. g., his preference for celibac temptation and turn now to the examination the context of the epistle as a whole and th

We suggest that those verses are better u printed this way:

8 TO THE UNMARRIED and to widow:

10 TO THE MARRIED *I give this ruling,*
      Lord's:
      a wife must not *SEPARATE* herself fr(

11   if she does, she must either remain un
      her husband;
      and the husband must not *DIVORCE*

12 TO THE REST *I say this, as my own* v
      if a Christian has a heathen wife, and sh
      he must not *DIVORCE* her;

13   and a woman who has a heathen husb
      must not *DIVORCE* her husband.

14   For the heathen husband now belongs t
      wife, and the heathen wife through he
      wise your children would not belong t
      do.

15   If on the other hand the heathen par
      TION, let him have it.
      In such cases the Christian husband
      sion; but God's call is a call to live

16   Think of it: as a wife you may be y
      as a husband you may l

who believed they were inspired by the living Christ. This possibility is explicitly stated in 1 Corinthians 11:23, which reads, "For the tradition which I handed on to you came to me from the Lord himself . . . ." [NEB] This alternative would explain why Paul does not purport to quote the historical Jesus and hence why we cannot easily match his words with those of Jesus preserved in the Gospels. It also allows us to understand that Paul did not claim to have special inspiration from the living Christ. That Paul is appealing to the church's tradition regarding the message of Christ seems the best way for us to understand the claim that his position is that of the "Lord."

Another issue that arises from this passage is Paul's use of the two words "separate" (*chōrizō*) and "divorce" (*aphiāmi*). In verse 10, with reference to wives, he prohibits separation; and in verse 15 he allows for a separation from an unbelieving spouse. But in verses 11, 12, and 13 he uses the word "divorce"—the husband must not divorce his wife; the husband of a non-Christian who is willing to live on with him should not divorce her; and similarly a Christian wife married to an unbeliever willing to continue the relationship should not divorce him. Now some have attempted to interpret this passage in the light of a distinction between these two words. They have proposed that "separation" as Paul intends it here does not refer to the legal dissolution of the marriage relationship. It means, according to some, a parting of the spouses without a formal divorce. It appears that Paul held that whereas the husband could *divorce* his wife (vs. 11), a wife could only *separate* from her husband (vs. 10).

Unfortunately such a proposed distinction between divorce and separation is not accurate. Paul does seem to employ them in a distinct way in verses 10 and 11. But in verses 12, 13, and 15 he uses the two terms interchangeably. In verse 12 he recognizes the right of the wife of an unbeliever to *divorce* (*aphiāmi*) her husband, and in verse 15 either spouse has the right to *separate* (*chōrizō*) from her or his non-Christian partner. Moreover, in verse 11, after counseling against a woman's separating from her husband, he exhorts that should she do so anyway she should remain single. Implicit in what Paul says in verse 11 is that what he means by separation is a legal dissolution of the marriage relationship, which allows the woman the possibility of remarrying. We agree with the conclusion reached by R. L. Roberts:

> To make a distinction between divorce and separation, as some have
> done, is not allowed by the meaning of *chōrizō* in the context of
> I Corinthians 7. No such distinction is made by Paul. . . . While *chōri-*
> *zō* is not the most frequently used word for divorce in the New Testament,
> it is referring here to the separation of divorce and is not speaking of mere
> separation with the marriage still binding. [R. L. Roberts, Jr., "The
> Meaning of *Chorizo* and *Douloo* in I Corinthians 7:10-17," *Restoration*
> *Quarterly* 8, no. 1 (1965): 182.]

Still another issue must be discussed before we move on to conclude what Paul says about divorce. The discussion in verses 12-16
calls to mind a Jewish practice. Jewish writings prohibited marriage
of Jews to foreign persons. Ezra 9:1-2 and 10:11 forbid Jewish men
to marry women from foreign countries and insist that where such
marriages have been contracted they be dissolved. There is a parallel
to some degree between what Paul advises in verses 12-16 and the
legislation of Ezra. In both cases the believer is bound in marriage to
an unbeliever. But the parallel is not absolute. In the case of the
marriage of Jewish men to foreign women, the union took place while
the Jew was a believer. In the case of the Christians Paul is addressing,
it appears that when the union was contracted both parties were
non-Christian. After the marriage union, one of the spouses has
become a Christian. Moreover, there is a distinction between the
counsel of Ezra and that of 1 Corinthians in the insistence upon the
separation. Ezra's word is absolute: "Separate yourselves from the
foreign population and from your foreign wives." Paul's words are
conditional: remain married if you desire, but if the unbeliever demands a divorce, grant it. The Jewish practice may have been in the
back of Paul's mind as he wrote verses 12-16, but he has altered it
considerably in the light of his Christian perspective.

We can now move closer to our specific concern. These issues we
have discussed are important to our study, but we must now try to
conclude what exactly Paul is saying.

First, it is obvious that he wants to forbid divorce. The husband
or the wife should not divorce their spouses (vss. 10 and 11). From
the Christian perspective, marriage to an unbeliever is not in itself
grounds for divorce (vs. 12). Paul's attitude seems clear—divorce is
not desirable for a Christian. What he says later in the chapter at verse
39 seems to summarize Paul's view of marriage and divorce: "A wife

is bound to her husband as long as he lives." Marriage is a permanent relationship.

Second, it is equally obvious that Paul desires to eliminate the possibility of remarriage. If divorce does occur, the woman (at least) should remain single (vs. 11). Divorce does not free one to remarry; only the death of a spouse opens up that possibility (vs. 39). In the next section we must investigate the logic of Paul's position on remarriage after divorce, but for now we can only note that position.

Third, on the other hand, Paul recognizes one exception to the prohibition against divorce. If the unbelieving partner desires a divorce, the Christian spouse should allow it (vs. 15). This exception to an otherwise absolute word against divorce inevitably calls to mind the passages in Matthew (5:32 and 19:9) where Jesus prohibits divorce unless the woman is guilty of adultery. In both Paul and Matthew we have an absolute prohibition against divorce quickly qualified with an exception. But how different the exceptions are in the two cases! For Matthew the exception is adultery. For Paul it is marriage to an unbeliever who wants out of the relationship. What can we make of this? We argued in the previous chapter that the absolute prohibition against divorce was the earliest form of the saying of Jesus. Matthew's exception entered into the tradition of the words of Jesus amid the practical situations in the early church and its efforts to interpret the traditional word of Jesus. In Paul's case we have a similar situation. Paul knows that the tradition contains the exhortation that divorce not be allowed. But in the concrete, real-life situations of the church, this is difficult. How can a Christian maintain a marriage with an unbelieving partner who desires to end the marriage? Paul's practical mind is at work in his interpretation of the word out of the tradition. He is bold in saying that while the ruling from the "Lord" is that there should be no divorce, in his own view there is at least one occasion when divorce may occur.

Matthew and Paul enable us to see how the early church did not take the words of Jesus as an absolute regulation. They practiced a certain "interpretative freedom." And they did so not out of any disregard for the message that the tradition claimed was the word of Jesus. They did so out of concern for the human lives of the Christians of their time. It seemed inhuman to Matthew and his community that a marriage should have to continue where the wife was guilty of adultery. It seemed inhuman to Paul that a marriage should have to continue where the unbelieving spouse wished a divorce from the Christian partner. The significance of this for our understanding is immeasurable: *what the early Christians (Paul and Matthew) did was to understand the word of Jesus not as an absolute regulation but as a word of guidance to be interpreted in the light of human welfare*. Matthew and Paul feel free to qualify the word of the tradition when such qualification is necessary for nurturing human welfare. If we may venture a generalization, both Matthew and Paul take a situationalist view of the prohibition against divorce. It is generally true that divorce is to be forbidden. But divorce may be necessary when the lives of persons are seriously threatened by the continuance of a marriage. We are, as Paul says, called to a life of peace, and in some circumstances that may require a divorce. We will return to this point in the concluding section of this chapter.

 Fourth, and finally, we must observe that there is a parallel between Paul's attitude and those Gospel sayings about divorce and remarriage which we concluded were most nearly like what Jesus himself might have said. You will recall that we emphasized the realism of the word of Jesus in (especially) the passage in Mark 10:11. Divorce is forbidden, but if it occurs there should be no remarriage. The word of Jesus acknowledges the fact of human failure. There will indeed be divorces in spite of the teaching that marriage is a permanent, spiritual union. Paul's realism is equally evident. It is expressed in 1 Corinthians 7:11. If divorce does occur, in spite of the injunction against it, let there be no remarriage. Paul, too, knows the power of humans to distort the ideal of marriage and to enter into relationships which cannot be the spiritual union that marriage is intended to be. Human sin is bound to result in the dissolution of some marriages. That realism is equally expressed in the point we made in the preceding paragraph. There are bound to be situations in which the prohibition against divorce cannot be sustained. So Paul—like Jesus—had no illusions about the capacity of humans to fulfill the intention of God for marriage. He knew that human sin affects the entire realm of personal and societal life.

Paul's Teachings on Divorce and Remarriage in the Context of His General Message

It is time now that we moved some distance away from the individual trees in order to get a view of the forest. It has been said already that the interpretation of Biblical texts must be done in a wholistic manner—that passages must be understood in the light of their context. We approached Paul's statements on divorce and remarriage in 1 Corinthians 7 only after discussing briefly the whole of the epistle and then the whole of the chapter. Now that we understand what Paul says about these questions in that chapter we must again return to the context. We must place those statements in the context, first, of his primary theological concern in the chapter and then in the context of some of the major themes of his theology expressed elsewhere in his epistles. For we are interested not just with the historical question of what Paul said. We are more concerned with what meaning his words may have for Christians living in this century. So we must first establish as best we can what it is he did say and then turn to the quest for understanding those words as guidance for us today. This latter step is one that requires seeing the whole forest of Paul's teaching and not becoming lost examining the bark of one of the trees in that forest.

When we ask what is the relevance of Paul's teaching on divorce and remarriage for present-day Christian practice, there are two themes in Paul's message we must keep in mind. The first theme appears in this same chapter. In our brief outline of 1 Corinthians 7 in the previous section, we noted that Paul invokes a general principle which he applies to the question of the relationship of the sexes. That principle, briefly stated, is that Christians should remain in the condition in which they were at the time of their conversion. Slaves should not seek to be free from their masters. Those who were circumcised should not attempt to have surgery done which would remove the marks of circumcision. Unmarried persons should remain single, if they can. Married persons should continue in that relationship, if at all possible. Paul's counsel sounds a conservative note. He does not believe that becoming a Christian should alter one's social status or condition. He urges the continuation of the social *status quo* for his readers.

But we must understand the reason for his articulation of this principle. It is not that he is endorsing the social *status quo*. He is not making a concession here to the world and its standards. He does not send Onesimus the slave back to his master Philemon because he endorses the institution of slavery (see the letter to Philemon). Paul *sounds* like a social conservative because of a particular theological view he held. His principle of remaining in the state in which you were called is a reflection of his eschatological view of things.

This principle, which seems so conservative to us, is based on Paul's firm conviction that the parousia (or the return) of Christ was soon to occur. It is very important that we understand Paul's eschatological motivation as he exhorts Christians to remain in whatever state they were called. He advised people to put up with their social status because he believed that the entire social realm—indeed the whole structure of the world—was about to be radically transformed. He makes this explicit in verses 29-31 of chapter 7: "The time we live in will not last long. . . . For the whole frame of this world is passing away." (vss. 29, 31, NEB) The same theme is announced in Romans 13:11-14. The time for the consummation of history is immediately upon us. The social relationships we now have will soon all be dissolved and an entirely new order installed with the realization of the kingdom of God. With Christ's return, all these present conditions of humans (slavery, circumcision, marriage, etc.) will be transformed.

It is not easy to illustrate the attitude of Paul on this matter. The finality of the parousia of Christ for the early Christians is perhaps most comparable to the sense of the finality of death. If a person knew that she was soon to die—let's say within a year—her entire perspective on her social condition would be transformed. The business deals which she might have under way at the moment would no longer be important. Her plans to marry and have children would very probably be put to one side. Many of the changes she planned in her condition (which were premised on a longer life) would lose their importance for her. The fact of her impending death would thrust everything into a new and drastically different light. Priorities would be radically readjusted. Perhaps the analogy is not entirely appropriate. But such a comparison does suggest the manner in which the impending return of Christ and the establishment of the kingdom of God affected Paul's attitude. His priorities were much different from what they might have been had he believed that the return of Christ was a far distant reality and that Christians had a role in a world history that would go on for several centuries after his time. Just as an imminent expectation of death transforms the view one takes of personal conditions, so the imminent expectation of an end to world history transformed Paul's view of social conditions.

Paul's eschatological view of history pervades his discussion in 1 Corinthians 7. Indeed, that eschatological perspective pervades much of his writings, as it does almost the whole of the New Testament. Paul was convinced that Christ would soon return, and this conviction conditioned his perspective on this world and its history. When the Christians at Thessalonica were influenced by a view that claimed Christ's return had already occurred, Paul strictly admonished them not to accept such a belief (2 Thess.). The return was imminent, Paul insisted, but had not yet occurred, since the radical changes he anticipated had not taken place. Except perhaps in his last epistles (e. g., portions of Philippians), Paul clung to this belief throughout his life. Indeed, the earliest Gospel materials seem to reflect the view that Jesus too had taught that the consummation of history was near. The early church held this view tenaciously, even when it posed problems for them. As the years passed and the parousia did not occur, there is evidence that it troubled the Christians (2 Peter 3:8-9). Only gradually did the early Christians begin to come to grips with the fact that the church was not simply a temporary community holding its breath until the full kingdom came with Christ's return. The two-volume work of Luke (the Gospel and Acts of the Apostles) was one effort to demonstrate how the church must accept its mission in the world as a more enduring body.It remained for the later church to work out a more complete understanding of the delay of the parousia. (However, the Gospel of John may have proposed the view that Christ's parousia occurred with his resurrection and the bestowal of the Spirit.)

Consequently, Paul's view of divorce and remarriage is conditioned by his expectation of the immediate return of Christ and the dissolution of all societal structures of this world. Indeed all of his views in 1 Corinthians 7 are premised on this eschatology. Clarence T. Craig has written,

> The whole chapter [1 Cor. 7] is dominated . . . by the expectation of the

imminent Parousia. Responsibility toward children and the generations to come does not enter into the apostle's calculations, for he thought of himself as living not in the first century but in the last century. Marriage was of doubtful wisdom because it might divert from undivided attention to the work of the Lord. ["I Corinthians, Exegesis," *The Interpreter's Bible,* ed. George A. Buttrick (New York: Abingdon Press, 1953), vol. 10, p. 76]

When we understand the importance of this expectation for the apostle and when we realize that his expectation was, at least, miscalculated, a question invariably is asked: are Paul's exhortations relevant for Christians living in the twentieth century? Does Paul's misunderstanding of the parousia render his pronouncements obsolete? We think that we should not go to the extreme with our answers to these questions. We do not have to mark off all of Paul's views in this chapter simply because he was wrong about the expected return of Christ. But we must honestly reevaluate them in the light of the dominant role of his eschatological views. Would Paul's view of divorce and remarriage have been different had he known that the social structures would not be transformed in his lifetime by the return of Christ?

It is possible to suggest some points at which Paul might have stuck to his views and some points at which he might have revised them. These are speculations, of course. But given the understanding we have gained of what Paul was driving at in this chapter, let's try to construct his position outside of the immediate eschatological expectation.

First, it is safe to say that his reservations about divorce would not be altered. We can discern that his view of divorce itself is based not upon the impending parousia alone. To be sure, his eschatological expectations did influence his view of divorce. Since one is to remain in his or her present condition until the return of Christ, according to Paul, that would mean remain married and do not seek a divorce. But his view of divorce, we must suppose, is also premised on his view of marriage as a lasting and permanent spiritual union of male and female. Therefore, he would still counsel the avoidance of divorce. This supposition is also supported by the fact that he believed the prohibition against divorce was not simply his opinion but that of the Lord.

But we can further speculate that Paul would have been more lenient with regard to exceptions in the divorce prohibition. Had he known that Christians would continue to live in a history that went on long after his lifetime, and that marriages would continue for the lifetimes of all his readers, Paul would, we believe, have made his interpretation of the Lord's word on divorce more thorough. We suggested above that Matthew and Paul both interpret the prohibition against divorce in the light of human welfare. Paul might have expanded those exceptions had it not been for his conviction that Christ would soon return. As it was, Paul thought every marriage could endure the short time until the parousia, with the possible exception of marriages to unbelievers. Let us assume two new conditions in the situation to which Paul addresses himself: First, he knows that the parousia will not occur in the immediate future. Second, he knows of other cases in which Christians are involved in hopeless marriages—ones destructive of personality and faith (as he knew that Christians married to unbelievers who desired divorce were in a hopeless and destructive relationship). If we grant these two conditions, we can safely conclude that Paul would have counseled exceptions to the divorce regulation beyond the one he mentions. Paul's compassion and his basic concern for the nurturing of human welfare would have allowed him to exercise still further his interpretative freedom with the commandment of the Lord. Paul's compassion is illustrated in the manner in which he encourages those who desire to marry to do so, even though he wished they would remain celibate like him. He was concerned that human welfare not be impaired by social status. In the epistle to Philemon we see that Paul did not want slavery to be injurious to the welfare of the slave Onesimus, even though, perhaps because of his eschatological view, he did not advocate the abolition of slavery.

We think, then, that Paul would not have altered his insistence that divorce violates God's will for marriage. But we think that he would have broadened the qualifications to the divorce regulation. And further, if he had not held that Christ was soon to return, we think there is another aspect of his teaching that might have been different. On the issue of remarriage, it is hard to believe that the apostle would have been so strict had he seen a longer future for world history ahead of his readers. His reasons for denying the possibility

of remarriage seem to have been two. First, it was part of the tradition
he had received concerning the words of Jesus. Second, it was part of
his insistence that Christians not alter their social status in the last
days before the parousia. He makes clear that in those last days not
even first marriages were to be encouraged (7:8-9). The single state is
far better for those about to witness the end of world history. Remove
that eschatological view of history, and we believe that Paul would
have again been more lenient. Why should we believe this? Primarily
because of Paul's basic theological conviction that persons are always
invited by God to become new creations. His doctrine of salvation
would have led Paul to a more understanding view of remarriage, had
he not been so influenced by his anticipation of Christ's return. But
we delay further discussion of this theme until we have had a chance
to examine his doctrine of salvation more fully.

And before we do that, let there be a final word said concerning
the speculation in which we have just asked you to indulge. Should
Paul have held a different eschatology, we think he would still have
admonished Christians not to divorce. But he would have been more
lenient regarding the conditions under which divorce was allowable
and regarding remarriage of divorced persons. Such a speculative
process in which we have just engaged perhaps seems groundless. But,
on the other hand, Biblical interpretation must not be content with
the mere written words. It must seek the spirit of the writer—his
major contentions, his primary perspective, and his dominant themes.
If we are to find the Biblical writings relevant to our Christian lives
in the twentieth century, we cannot be content with even an enlightened literalism. Again, it is Jesus' attitude toward the Jewish law
which instructs us. He sought to find the inner meaning of the letter
of the law and to urge that meaning. He was not a literalist when it
came to the Torah. He said he was not concerned to destroy the law
but to fulfill it (Matt. 5:17). It is that kind of interpretive process of
seeking the inner meaning of Paul that we have attempted in these last
pages. In trying to discern what Paul would have taught had he not
been caught up in the expectation of an imminent parousia, we have
been seeking not to destroy Paul's word but to fulfill the spirit of his
words. We must honestly admit that Paul had misunderstood the
eschatological hope. The immediate return of Christ that Paul expected did not occur. But rather than dismissing Paul's words as

entirely obsolete because of his eschatology, we have taken another route. We have attempted to complete his words now in the light of a different eschatological vision.

This leads us to the consideration of Paul's words on divorce and remarriage in a still broader context. We have examined those words in the context of his conviction about the impending parousia in 1 Corinthians 7. Now we must examine his words in the context of his view of salvation and of justification by faith expressed in several of his epistles. The thesis of the exposition that follows is simply this: Paul's view of justification (or salvation) necessitates that one take a different view of divorce and remarriage from that in 1 Corinthians 7 when read in isolation.

Paul's ingenious insight into the gospel was that humans are not brought into right relationship with God through fulfilling the demands of the law, but by faith in the act of God's grace expressed in Christ. Paul was perhaps the first to see so clearly what a radical revelation of God was to be found in Christ. He saw that Christ's life, death, and resurrection meant that a whole new way of relating to God was offered to humans. One is not, Paul argued, brought into a harmonious relationship with God through obedience to the law. Humans need not prove by their works that they are lovable and acceptable to God. Humans need not make the laborious climb up the ladder of good works in order to be brought into the presence of God. As a matter of fact, Paul perceived that all such efforts were in themselves assertions of human pride which automatically rendered them failures. To attempt to make oneself acceptable to God through obedience to the law was already a gross assertion of human pretense. Possibly this is what Paul means by his statement, "What the law could never do, because our lower nature robbed it of all potency, God has done." (Rom. 8:3, NEB) Paul here seems to recognize the possibility that obedience to the law could bring one into right relationship with God. Hence he has a high regard for the law in and of itself (Rom. 7:12). But humans distort the law and deprive it of its power to bring them into a relationship with God. What Paul calls "our lower nature" is the presumption that humans are good enough to obey the law. Paul saw that when people attempt to use the law as a means of righting their relationship with God they have already committed a major sin. That sin is a form of pride in one's human capacity. And that sin alienates people from God no matter how faithful to the law they might be. So Paul is forced to the conclusion that " 'no human being can be justified in the sight of God' for having kept the law." (Rom. 3:2, NEB) Paul seems to have held a basic reservation about the human capacity to keep the law without an accompanying sin of pride. He held this reservation, apparently, because of his own personal experience with the law to which he witnesses in Romans 7.

Paul apparently conceived the law as a means by which humans attempt to right the relationship between themselves and God. Hence, it was the human approach to God, based on human ability to keep the law. A diagram now will permit us a better understanding later:

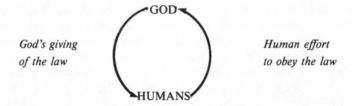

God's giving
of the law

Human effort
to obey the law

In Christ, Paul claims, a whole new way of correcting the relationship between humans and God has come into being. To return to Romans 8:3, he claims that what the law could not do because of the distortive nature of human pride, God has done for us. In the Christ event ("by sending his own Son in a form like that of our own sinful nature . . . so that the commandment of the law may find fulfilment in us" [8:3, NEB]) God has bypassed the law. He has declared that human sin is wiped out, abolished, pardoned. This is an act of his grace alone. It is not by human effort that the alienation between humans and God has been overcome. It is solely by an act of God's own grace—an act of God's own righteousness, not human righteousness. Acceptance by God is not contingent upon human effort, but solely on what God has done. It remains then for the human only to accept the acceptance offered by God in Christ. To accept the right relationship with God offered by him in Christ is to have faith in his offer.

Paul expounds all of this in Romans in terms of God's justice.

What he means by God's justice is God's willingness to do what must be done to bridge the gap of alienation between himself and humans. The apostle writes to the Romans, "God's justice has been brought to light. . . . it is God's way of righting wrong, effective through faith in Christ for all who have such faith . . . and all are justified by God's free grace alone, through his act of liberation in the person of Christ Jesus." (3:21-24, NEB) The way of the law, as a means of righting the relationship with God, has been replaced by the way of grace:

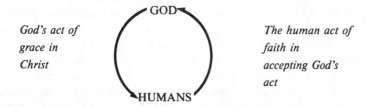

God's act of
grace in
Christ

The human act of
faith in
accepting God's
act

Christians must not, therefore, resort once again to the law as a means of finding acceptance in God's eyes. To do so, Paul argues, is to fall away from the heart of the gospel. In Galatians he argues that to depend upon the law in any way for one's salvation is to deny the effectiveness of faith in God's grace. He becomes very angry with those who have led the Christians in Galatia to think that obeying the law is the way to salvation. He calls the Galatians "stupid" for having been misled (Gal. 3:1, NEB), and declares that those who have misled his readers should be cast out (1:9). The Christian is free from the law as a means of overcoming sin (2:16). The law was useful as a "tutor" until God's revelation in Christ, but now "the tutor's charge is at an end." (3:24-25, NEB)

There are many problems involved in interpreting Paul's teachings regarding the law and justification by faith. Certainly our summary of those teachings is oversimplified and all too brief. But it is enough for us to see the thrust of Paul's radically new vision. It is enough for us to understand Paul's essential concept of the gospel and its meaning, so that we can proceed to discuss his teachings regarding divorce and remarriage in the light of that concept. We must ask now what it means to view these issues of divorce and remarriage in the context of Paul's general teaching about justification by faith.

First, it is obvious that Paul would have to say that observance of the divorce and remarriage regulation is not a matter of salvation. Since Paul denied that law was the means of righting our relationship with God, it follows that obedience to the laws regarding divorce and remarriage cannot be prerequisites for salvation. Those laws, just as all other laws, are not part of the means by which Christians are called upon to win God's approval. To argue otherwise would be to fall into the trap which Paul believed ensnared the Galatians. To take on any law as a condition for salvation is to move back into the "law way" of seeking salvation. Hence, the divorce and remarriage laws must not be viewed as absolute regulations upon which human salvation depends.

Second, Paul believed that sin was pardoned by God's grace alone. This means that Christians view themselves as sinners forgiven by God and reinstated in God's favor by virtue of that divine grace exhibited in Christ. To become entangled in a destructive and hopeless marital relationship and to seek release from it by means of a divorce is sin. It is to violate God's intention for marriage and the relationships of persons in marriage. But like all sin, the sin of marital failure and divorce is pardoned already by God's grace. This sin is no different from any other human act or attitude that alienates one from God. It is simply another expression of the human inclination to distort God's creation and misdirect one's own life. But, equally, it is no different from any other human sin in that it has been forgiven by God's just and righteous nature. Therefore, we must conclude that Paul held the sin of failure in marriage to be pardoned by God's grace in Christ.

Third, the pardon and love of God expressed in Christ meant for humans a new beginning. Paul spoke of it as a new creation (2 Cor. 5:17; Gal. 6:15). He uses the analogy of dying and rising with Christ to express the radically new beginning available in Christian faith (Rom. 6:3-4). God's act in Christ allows one to shed the garments of one's past and to be clothed in garments of a new future (Col. 3:10). The forgiveness of God puts to death one's sin in the past and opens up the possibility of a new future. The gospel is the good news of an open future—a future that is not burdened with the past and shaped by what has been. The future is shaped rather by God's love, not by past human failures.

The conclusion is inevitable that this view has something concrete to say about the possibility of remarriage following divorce. Paul's message logically implies that the failure of a past marriage can be buried in God's forgiveness and that the promise of a new beginning may properly lead to a second marriage. It would be untrue to Paul's central message to deny that this is the meaning of God's grace for the marital relationship. That one who has suffered a serious failure in marriage must be forever denied the opportunity of another relationship is to deny the power of God's grace to re-create the future. As a matter of fact, a Christian who has been divorced and is now remarried is one of the best living examples of the manner in which God's forgiveness can produce a new beginning. The process of divorce and remarriage among some persons is comparable to a death and resurrection. The dissolution of the old marriage is a painful death. There is regret, remorse, and guilt. When forgiveness is appropriated, there is an equally intense feeling of a new future. Remarriage is often an expression of the confidence of persons in the death of the past failure and the birth of a new, bright beginning. Those who have intimately known Christians who have struggled with a divorce and then found a new relationship with another spouse can testify that the experience is a form of human death and rebirth.

It is necessary for us to conclude then that Paul's central message is one that indeed allows for the opportunity of a second chance in marriage. Again for the sake of sound Biblical interpretation let us speculate a bit. If Paul had had occasion to think more fully about the matter of remarriage for Christians, he might well have come to the conclusion we have reached. His conviction regarding the nature of the Christian gospel might have led him to such a conclusion. We cannot fault Paul for not having articulated this implication of the gospel. He was still wrestling with the central theme of his message —searching for ways to express and better understand it. He was not confronted (except among the Corinthians) with the question of remarriage (or, at least his letters do not indicate that he was). But the spirit of Paul's vision of the gospel brings us to the view that where divorce is experienced as sin, where God's forgiveness is sought and accepted in faith for that sin, the possibility of remarriage emerges as a concrete expression of what it means to be a new creation as a result of God's grace.

Summary and Conclusions regarding Paul's Teachings on Divorce and Remarriage

Let us now look at where we have been and what destination we have reached. In 1 Corinthians 7:10-16 Paul repeats what he understands to be the command of the Lord regarding divorce and remarriage. That command is an exhortation not to divorce and not to remarry if divorce occurs. We found here the same realism that characterized the words of Jesus in the Gospels. Divorce is a violation of God's intention for marriage, but it will occur. But Paul also engages in a kind of interpretive freedom with regard to these words. Like Matthew he suggests that there is an exception to the prohibition on divorce, and like Matthew his exception is made out of concern for persons. The regulation regarding divorce and remarriage is not taken by Paul to be an absolute law but as a word of guidance to be interpreted in the light of human welfare.

When we placed Paul's words in the context of his general message in 1 Corinthians 7 and elsewhere in his epistles, some interesting facts emerged. It was seen how his expectation of the impending return of Christ conditioned his view of the relationship between the sexes. We attempted to understand the spirit of Paul's words, as best we could, by abstracting them from his eschatological view. Our conclusions were that he would continue to be opposed to divorce, but would have been more lenient with regard to the conditions under which divorce was permissible. Moreover, we concluded that his eschatological views might have influenced him to be more strict about remarriage than he might have been otherwise. Placed in the context of his message of justification by faith, Paul's teachings lead to quite a different conclusion. It seems that his understanding of God's grace and forgiveness might well have led him to accept divorce as *a human sin forgiven by God.* And if that is the case, then it surely follows that he would have to view remarriage, in some cases, as an expression of the new beginning bestowed upon the forgiven sinner.

Our examination of the issues of divorce and remarriage here has followed the same pattern as in the previous chapter. We studied the words of Jesus on divorce and remarriage found in the Gospels, and then placed them in the context of this general message. With Paul we have followed the same route. The results are similar. Both Paul and Jesus seem to view divorce as a violation of God's intention for marriage. Divorce and remarriage deny the spiritual union that God desires for husband and wife. However, both Paul and Jesus stress generally the fact of God's radical love and forgiveness. Both contend that where there is a violation of God's intention for marriage—where God's creation is distorted by human failure—there is sin, but sin that is pardoned by the love of God. Both stress that divorce and remarriage are never the original desire of God. But both emphasize that God is one who pardons the alienating acts of humans and invites them into a new life with a bright future shaped by his love. Between the concept of God as loving and accepting in the Gospels and the concept of the righteousness of God in Paul's epistles there is no irreconcilable difference. There is a different medium of expression. We find Jesus in the Gospels expressing this message in figurative language—parables most often—and with his own life-style. In Paul's letters we find the message expressed in more abstract concepts (e. g., the righteousness of God) and in theological constructions. But in both cases the point is the same. And we must say the same for the other side of the coin. What we called the radical demands of God in the Gospels find their expression, too, in Paul's words. He issues commands and injunctions which he takes to be God's will for human existence. Thus both Jesus and Paul have a vision of what God desires for human life, but both have an equally clear vision of God's willingness to accept and forgive the humans who thwart that divine desire.

Thus far we have discussed the Old Testament regulation regarding divorce and the words of Jesus and the words of Paul on divorce and remarriage. It remains for us to ask now what the relevance of the Biblical message, as we have come to understand it, is for the questions of divorce and remarriage in our society. How should the Christian view these matters today, and how should the church minister to divorced and possibly remarried persons? Can we be true to the Biblical witness in dealing with these issues in our society? To these and related questions we now turn.

4

THE ASUNDERED RECONCILED
The Ministry of the Church
to Divorced and Remarried Persons

Often it is easy to take a machine apart. It is simple to disassemble it into its smallest parts and to examine each of those parts individually. And there is something very satisfying about doing that. But the real test of skill comes when one must begin to put the pieces back together. To re-create the whole after having dismantled it is—even for the mechanically skilled—much more difficult.

We must turn now to perhaps the most difficult portion of our study. We have systematically disassembled the Biblical teachings on divorce and remarriage. We have isolated the Old Testament teaching in Deuteronomy 24:1-4 and examined it with some care. We have taken the synoptic sayings about divorce and remarriage apart and subjected them to the scrutiny of critical study. We have lifted out the divorce and remarriage saying of Paul in 1 Corinthians and viewed it from numerous angles in the light of the Christian gospel. But the time has come for putting the pieces together again. We know more now about the individual parts of the complicated question of the Biblical teachings on divorce and remarriage. So, when we have reassembled them and are able to look at the totality once again, we should be able to see the whole in a more understanding way. A person goes through the process of disassembling the engine of a car and putting it back together again for one important purpose. Having completed that process, she or he knows how the engine works. We can only hope that the process of disassembling the Biblical teachings on divorce and remarriage has given us new insights into how the individual parts of those teachings operate within the whole.

Our task in this chapter is twofold: First, we must try to offer some conclusion from our study of the Biblical teachings on our subject. Second, we must take the results of our inquiry and attempt to apply them to the ministry of the church to persons who are divorced and possibly remarried. In both sections we want to be as specific and practical as we can without violating the complexity of the subject.

Conclusions of Our Study

It may be helpful to summarize and try to elucidate some of the points of our earlier chapters.

First, the New Testament presents us with a clear prohibition against divorce and remarriage, based on the divine intention for marriage expressed in Genesis 2. What has become clear is that the prohibition against divorce and remarriage roots in a vision of what God desires of marriage. The New Testament material in this case takes its stand clearly upon an understanding of the Old Testament's declaration in the second creation story. Marriage is a divine institution originated by God. The intention of that institution is that male and female realize a spiritual union. Therefore, the union visualized for marriage is an indissoluble kind. It is such a thorough merging of the two personalities into one life that disjunction is unimaginable. It is like the union of the ingredients for a cake. Once they are mixed together into the cake dough, it is inconceivable that they may once again be separated into their individual parts.

The resistance to divorce expressed in the words of Jesus and confirmed in the teachings of the apostle Paul is founded on this understanding of the institution of marriage. That resistance makes no sense apart from its premise in the Genesis vision of the creation of marriage. This is an important point to understand. The denial of divorce has no basis in and of itself; it is a senseless and arbitrary regulation if it is lifted off its foundation in Genesis 2. It is not the acts of divorce or remarriage themselves that constitute the offense. It is those acts when viewed in the light of a vision of what marriage should be. The dissolution is not offensive unless one understands that the union itself is indissoluble.

This understanding of the Biblical prohibition against divorce and remarriage has a couple of important implications. First, it is obvious that the forbidding of divorce cannot be accepted where there is doubt regarding the truthfulness of the Genesis view of marriage. You cannot enforce a law where the premise of the law is unacceptable. Among those who do not believe that marriage is the kind of union described in Genesis, it is foolish to expect that the prohibition against divorce will be honored. This matter finds a parallel in present-day society. The strict and perhaps harsh penalties for possession and use of marihuana are premised on the conviction that the use of that material is seriously destructive of the human body and personality. But those who don't believe marihuana is destructive don't obey the law. Prohibition may be readily accepted only where there is acceptance of the basis of the prohibition.

The rise in divorce rates in America may in part be due to an ignorance or rejection of the Biblical teachings. Perhaps many do not understand or know the basis of the Biblical prohibition against divorce—what God intended marriage to be. Marriage is seldom viewed today in our secular society as a divine institution in which a permanent union of two personalities is realized. Marriage has been for the most part "desacralized." That is, marriage is viewed less and less as a divine institution with the divine goal of spiritual union. Instead, it is viewed as a convenient arrangement for two individuals who at the time find their lives compatible. The goal of marriage in our society, secularized as it is, is not spiritual union but happy harmony. The practical point of this argument is simply this: if the church wants to diminish the practice of divorce effectively in our society, it should attack not divorce itself and those who are divorced. It should, rather, propagate its vision of marriage which logically makes divorce unnecessary. This, however, gets us ahead of our story, and we postpone further discussion of that need until later in the chapter.

The thrust of this argument is that the divorce regulation when analyzed logically seems more intended to nurture a proper concept of marriage than to deny the possibility of divorce. It is the responsibility of the church to rethink the matter of divorce in the light of that view of marriage and in the light of a realistic view of human nature. With that we are brought to our second conclusion.

Second, there is throughout the Biblical teachings a realism regarding the human capacity for achieving the divine intention for marriage. We have met that realism in the course of each of the three segments of our journey through the Biblical material. In the Old Testament we found it to be simply accepted that some marriages will fail. The potential for human failure in marriage is taken for granted throughout the Old Testament. The result is that all the Old Testament

teachings on divorce and remarriage seek to do is
greatest possible degree of justice and propriety in div
riage. The synoptic sayings of Jesus show that realism
ever divorces his wife . . . .' " (Mark 10:11) While Jesus view
indissolubility of marriage as the ideal, he nonetheless implied that the
ideal is not always going to be realized. The human power for distorting God's intention is too great for Jesus not to recognize that marital
breakdowns are going to occur. The apostle Paul reflects almost precisely the same view: "a wife must not separate herself from her
husband; *if she does,* she must either remain unmarried or be reconciled to her husband." (1 Cor. 7:10-11, NEB, emphasis added) Again,
Paul acknowledges that many couples will never achieve the genuine
purpose of marriage.

We have tried to view this realism in the context of the total
Biblical realism about human existence. Throughout the Biblical witness is the concept that people distort and disobey the original structures of existence. It is not surprising then that the Biblical teachings
on divorce acknowledge this possibility for human shortcoming. It is
instructive that the ideal of God's intention for marriage is placed
alongside this hard realism. We would expect one or the other—either
the ideal, or the hard reality. But the Biblical material confronts us
with both placed side by side. The point of that coupling of the ideal
and the reality is important. It means that the Bible could teach both
the goal of human marriage and at the same time recognize that some
men and women will fail to reach that goal. Why can the church of
today not practice the same harmony of idealism and reality?

But this theme of Biblical realism necessitates that we reiterate
here a subpoint which we have encountered in our study. The failure
of a marriage to realize the spiritual union described in Genesis 2 must
be acknowledged as an evidence of sin. Now we want to use this worn
and weary term *sin* in its best theological sense. We mean by it that
state of being, experienced by humans, which alienates them from
God and consequently alienates them from other humans and from
themselves. The failure of the marriage of a man and a woman to
achieve the kind of relationship intended for the institution of marriage can only be viewed as an expression of the fundamental kind of
brokenness in humanity to which the Christian faith has always
pointed. The dissolution of a marriage is sin. Not sin in the simple

sense of having done something wrong. Not sin in the sense of doing the "no-no." But sin in the sense of the human predicament of distorting God's original intention for life. The Biblical injunctions force upon us the recognition that divorce is part of the total human mis orientation and fallenness. This means, however, that not only divorce itself but every failure of marriage to realize God's purpose is sinful. The couple that lives together without progress toward spiritual union, but struggles on in a destructive relationship afraid of the act of divorce, is failing as surely as the couple that separates with divorce. The couple that hides their marital failure behind a social facade for whatever reason (the children, what others would think, fear, etc.) have equally failed to achieve the purpose of God for marriage. While we must openly and clearly declare that divorce is an expression of human sinfulness, we must not stop there. We must declare just as openly and just as clearly that any marital relationship short of progress toward the spiritual union of the couple is likewise an expression of human failure.

Biblical realism forces us to acknowledge that marital breakdown is an instance of human sin. But the Biblical treatment of this reality also makes clear that marital failure is only one among many instances of human sinfulness. Nowhere in our study do we find the injunctions against divorce and remarriage suggesting that these violations of God's creative intention are more serious than any others. One writer has observed with displeasure that divorce is viewed in the contemporary church as if it were the "unpardonable sin" (Dwight Hervey Small, *The Right to Remarry* [Old Tappan, N.J.: Fleming H. Revell Co., 1975], p.12). Our investigation has produced no evidence that such a view can be supported on Biblical grounds. Everywhere the failure in marriage is viewed simply as another among many instances of human failure. If remarriage after divorce is called adulterous, so is the lustful glance (Matt. 5:28). The church has no Biblical justification for looking upon divorce and remarriage as "more sinful" than other acts or attitudes or feelings. Biblical realism must be newly appropriated by the church if it is to minister effectively and faithfully to persons who have suffered divorce and perhaps have chosen to remarry. We may, moreover, be guided by another closely related theme in the Biblical teachings. That theme is our next conclusion.

Third, there is throughout the Biblical teachings on divorce and remarriage a concern for the humanization of social practices. The Bible encourages a view of marriage which takes as the goal of marital relationships the union of the couple. Hence, it forbids that divorce be allowed to violate that spiritual union. But it teaches that the human capacity for distorting divine intention is so great that marital failure is bound to occur. Therefore it seeks to control the way in which that failure is treated in social practices. It is concerned throughout the passages we have examined to humanize divorce and remarriage customs. Biblical realism is accompanied by Biblical humanization.

The Old Testament is the best example of this tendency toward the humanization of divorce and remarriage practices. We saw in our study that every passage in the Old Testament dealing with divorce and remarriage (in any way other than metaphorically) had humanization as its intent. The legislative passages as well as the prophetic passage were designed to bring justice and fairness into the common practices of the Hebrew society. Now, from our twentieth-century perspective, we may wish that the Old Testament had gone further than it does in this direction. We might wish, for instance, that it had insisted upon the equality of women in matters of divorce and remarriage. But we cannot argue with the tendency which it exhibits. Divorce and remarriage are going to occur; the Hebrew people were hardheaded realists and could not deny this fact. What they sought to do then was to bring the manner in which those occurrences took place into greater harmony with the will of the just and righteous God they worshiped. They correctly perceived that their God was identified with the "losers" in life—the oppressed, the hurt, and the shattered persons.

The words of Jesus in the synoptic Gospels and the teachings of Paul both continue this basic Old Testament theme. We have suggested that one of the possible reasons for Jesus' objections to the practice of divorce in his day was that he so clearly saw that practice as oppressive and dehumanizing. The apostle Paul was concerned to discourage divorce if possible. But he was also concerned with the welfare of those caught in impossible marital relationships, and he tried to allow for the most just and humane resolution possible.

The Biblical teachings on divorce and remarriage seem to acknowledge the terrible injustice liable in marital dissolution. The Bible seems to know that divorce can be one of the most dehumanizing and shattering experiences of social life. We have only to read between the lines a bit to uncover this sensitivity to the vulnerability of persons in the midst of marital disorder. And to no one's surprise! For is not the Bible throughout a testimony to divine concern for the pain and suffering that humans cause for themselves within social structures? The announcement of God to Moses in the book of Exodus epitomizes the concern of the Biblical God for the human plight:

> The LORD said, "I have indeed seen the misery of my people in Egypt. I have heard their outcry against their slave-masters. I have taken heed of their sufferings, and have come down to rescue them from the power of Egypt." [Ex. 3:7-8, NEB]

The concern of God for the suffering of the people of Israel in slavery in Egypt is illustrative of his concern for human suffering throughout the Biblical witness. The desire to ease the suffering of marital breakdown is of a piece with the total view of God in the Biblical material.

The church may again be guided by this Biblical theme. Whatever else the church can do about divorce and remarriage in our society, it needs to work actively to humanize the practices of our day. It must continue and further the concern of the Hebrew people, of Jesus, and of Paul that marital suffering be minimized and that the rights of the oppressed be protected. This encompassing theme means a great many things which we cannot develop here in detail. But we must note that the tendency toward humanization is reflected in still another theme we found in the New Testament sections of our study.

Fourth, we saw that the prohibition against divorce and remarriage was subjected to interpretive freedom in the early church. Jesus' strict word about divorce which arose out of his dialogue with religious leaders of his day prohibits divorce on the grounds of the view of marriage found in Genesis. But we found in our study that that strict prohibition was very early interpreted freely by Christians. First, we found that Matthew (and/or his church) eases the strictness of the prohibition with his exception clause—divorce is forbidden except in the case of adultery (Matt. 5:32 and 19:9). Then we found Paul following suit. Divorce is to be discouraged except when a believer finds him or herself wedded to an unbeliever who desires a divorce (1 Cor. 7:15).

We think we have demonstrated that these exceptions to the strict prohibition are rooted in a common basis. In both cases, the exceptions are made out of concern for the welfare of the persons involved. The theme of humanization that we have discussed above, therefore, came to expression in the freedom which Matthew (and his church) and Paul exercised in applying the prohibition to actual situations. There are two points which must be drawn from this result of our study.

1. The early Christians did not attempt to make the words of Jesus into absolute, inviolable law for their lives. They did not understand the word of Jesus to be binding upon them in every situation. Rather, they took that exhortation as a guide for their practice. It pointed them in a direction. It laid out a path which they might follow. But it did not bind them inescapably. Nowhere in the New Testament do we find Jesus' words taken to be a new law to be absolutely obeyed. Nowhere, except perhaps in the Gospel of Matthew. That Gospel seems to present the teachings of Jesus as a "new Torah" and Jesus himself as the "new Moses, the law-giver." Yet it is precisely in Matthew that we find the freedom to interpret the teachings of Jesus exemplified in the matter of divorce. We must conclude that the early Christians did *not* understand the revelation of God in Christ to be the revelation of absolute law which they must obey faithfully in order to win salvation. The modern Christian must assimilate this insight. The teachings of Jesus are not religious law. But most especially the modern Christian must appropriate this view with regard to the divorce and remarriage prohibition. Nowhere else, perhaps, is the tendency toward a modern Christian legalism more evident than in the case of divorce and remarriage. The bulk of the New Testament argues against a religious legalism in general. And our study has shown that there is no New Testament foundation for a legalistic stance regarding divorce and remarriage.

2. We need to draw another point from the fact that early Christians exercised an interpretive freedom in relationship to Jesus' prohibition against divorce. The application of the exhortation against divorce is controlled by one principle in Matthew and Paul. That is the principle of human welfare. This means simply that divorce and remarriage regulations must be subjected to a fundamental care for human personality. This seems to be such a simple point that it hardly

needs elucidation. Yet too often contemporary Christian attitudes tend to subject the human person to the divorce and remarriage regulation rather than the regulation to the person. Jesus declares that the sabbath was made for the sake of humans and not humans for the sake of the sabbath (Mark 2:27). That declaration holds within itself the principle that Matthew and Paul applied to the divorce and remarriage regulation. The law, Jesus said, was designed to further and enhance human welfare. That was the whole purpose of the sabbath regulation. We must not then turn it upon its head with the result that humans become enslaved to still another master—in this case the law concerning the sabbath.

Marriage was made for humans; not humans for marriage. Therefore, when marriage fails to enhance and further the total well-being of the humans involved, it must be dissolved. The injunction against divorce must not be enforced with a strictness that results in the destruction of human personality and potential. It is a simple matter of values. Which is more important—the continuance of a legal marital bond or the happiness and nurture of the two humans involved? The New Testament material we have looked at, plus the general thrust of the Biblical witness, leave no doubt as to where the Bible stands on this question. The divorce regulation was made for human well-being—to protect and nurture marriage as a spiritual union of the couple. Humans must not be enslaved to the letter of that regulation. We can do no better than to cite the revolutionary idea of the apostle Paul that the very essence of the gospel is the liberation of humans from subjection to law of any and every kind.

Consequently, contained within the acts of Matthew and Paul in reinterpreting the prohibition against divorce is the very heart of the gospel and of our study. Christianity is a religion of grace and not law; and it is a religion that frees persons from the oppressive nature of legalistic systems of all sorts. And with that affirmation we are brought to the last concluding statement of our survey of the Biblical material.

Finally, there is a necessary and inescapable tension between God's creative intent for humanity and his redemptive intent. Most especially in the recorded teachings of Jesus is that tension evident. But it also moves below the surface of the Pauline material. On the one hand, there is the announcement of the will of God for human existence.

That announcement paints a picture of humanity living harmoniously with the desire of God for his creation. It vividly portrays the meaning of absolute obedience to the intention of God for persons and nature as a whole. Part of that divine intent was that marriage be the spiritual union of male and female unassailable by all of the separating and destructive forces loose in the universe. It is that divine intention that Jesus' so-called ethical teachings were designed to articulate. They were designed to present human life as it might be conceived under the full reign of God. The kingdom of God about which Jesus spoke so frequently is nothing other than the restoration of creation to its Creator.

But on the other hand, the teachings of Jesus and the writings of Paul declare with equal force the redemptive, forgiving and re-creating intention of God. The restoration of the creation to its Creator is accomplished in a startling way: the acceptance of the love of the Creator for his creatures. It is not restored by the announcement of the creative intention of God as a new law. It is restored by the process of embracing more and more fully the forgiveness and acceptance of God. So the redemptive act of God in Christ is the good news that no person need be excluded from a harmonious relationship with the Creator. No matter what offense has been committed. No matter how little the reign of God has been allowed to prevail in a human life. No matter how much we have alienated the creation from its Creator. The way of restoration is through loving acceptance which places humanity back in relationship with God.

The redemptive intention of God is sheer folly to the human mind (1 Cor. 1:21-31). Many of us would take the expression of the divine will and enforce it with a vengeance until it was finally universally realized. But such worldly means are not God's means. He would instead announce to humans that they are loved and accepted as they are, regardless of the ethical quality of their lives. It is no wonder then that we have had difficulty in understanding that the violation of God's intention for marriage is forgivable and acceptable to God. It is no wonder that we have tried to transform the words of Jesus into a new law regarding divorce and remarriage. The radical nature of God's redemptive manner is not easy for us to comprehend. It evades us in spite of our constant effort to grasp it anew.

But what the New Testament declares is that God's redemptive

plan is at work, and we are enlisted into that plan. As we have been
reconciled by God's love, we are asked to become reconcilers (2 Cor.
5:18-20). What this means for divorce and remarriage should be
evident. It means that the forgiving love of God accepts into fellowship with him those persons who have experienced the failure of
marriage. The human sin which has occasioned the dissolution of the
marriage relationship is forgiven. And with that forgiveness comes
freedom from the past and for the future. This means that the divorced person is pointed toward the future with the promise that there
are to be new beginnings and new opportunities. Having been forgiven
his or her past, the divorced individual is granted another opportunity
to achieve the goal of marriage in a new relationship.

Through all of this divine intention for creation is not lost. It is
not simply relegated to a secondary place below the redemptive will
of God. Rather, it functions in a constant dialectic with the redemptive will of God. It brings us to the realization of our need for God's
grace. It points us toward what it means to live a new life under the
shelter of God's love. The two—the intention of God in creation and
the intention of God in redemption—function like the two tracks of
a stereo sound system. Each produces its theme, coming at the individual from two different directions but together blending into one
full and complete production.

The church has never grasped the full impact of what it means to
be a people of God under his grace. Often the church's actions speak
louder than its words that it does not live by grace but is constantly
pulled back into a life of oppressive law. While the preaching of the
church may announce the good news of God's grace, the sound of
those words is too often drowned out by the noise of the way the
church acts. (See the provocative and prophetic book by William
Hordern, *Living by Grace* [Philadelphia: The Westminster Press,
1975].) Not least the church has failed for the most part to practice
grace in relationship to the reality of divorce and remarriage in our
society. It has allowed itself to take the will of God for marriage and
make of it a law which thwarts the reality of grace. Divorced persons
have not been, in many cases, received in a "gracious" way by the
community of faith, but have been met instead by the condemnation
of the law forbidding divorce. The intent of God for creation and the
intent of God for redemption may be viewed as the two wings of a

bird which work together to allow the bird to soar above the earth. The church's attitude toward the divorced person sometimes reminds one of the poor bird that tries to fly with only one wing. It flaps its one wing vigorously, but can succeed only in hopping along on the ground. Until the church can get beyond merely articulating God's plan and actually *practice* the grace of the gospel, it shall not soar above earthly standards to a reconciling and healing ministry to the asundered of our society.

The Ministry of the Church to Divorced and Possibly Remarried Persons

But how is this to be done? How can the church proclaim at once the will of God that marriage be permanent and at the same time extend the forgiving grace of God to those who have experienced the dissolution of marriage? It is in part at least the old question of how the church offers forgiveness without implying approval of the wrong that has been committed. How does the church fly with both wings —God's will for creation and his redemptive grace? In the section just completed we have anticipated some of what we believe must be said on this subject. But more specificity is required. In the light of our study of the Biblical teachings on divorce and remarriage, what proposals can be made for the ministry of the church? We shall try to become as specific as possible in the space we have, and offer five proposals. We do not want to appear so presumptuous as to instruct the church in what it should do; but we do believe that these proposals for action arise directly from the study we have just completed. Hence, we offer them for your consideration.

The church needs to articulate more clearly and frequently a view of marriage based on Genesis 2. This proposal for action involves a number of subproposals. First, such an articulation as we propose must begin with a rethinking of the Christian view of marriage. We cannot develop this reformulation in detail here. But we would like to propose a brief outline of the shape such a reformulation might take. We would particularly like to suggest some ways in which the unity of marriage mentioned in Genesis 2 might be understood today.

Genesis 2:24 is an elusive passage. Originally the expression "the two become one flesh" may have meant a physical union. It might have referred to the act of sexual intercourse in which the flesh of the couple becomes in a sense one. Such a meaning would suggest the high regard the Hebrew people had for human sexuality. (See Gerhard von Rad, *Old Testament Theology* [New York: Harper & Row, 1962], vol. I, p. 150.) But this literal meaning of the passage is transcended by another possible meaning. The act of sexual intercourse may be a symbolic expression of another sense of unity. It can symbolize, in some cases, the sense in which the two lives of the husband and wife have become so interrelated that a single unity emerges from their individuality. The oneness of the husband and wife consists not of physical reality, however, but of their relationship. In this case, the oneness is found in the interplay of the two personalities. While the word "flesh" (*basar*) often means all animal and human life together (e. g., Gen. 7:21), it is also used in the Old Testament to refer to human life alone (e. g., Num. 16:22; Isa. 40:6). Therefore the two becoming one "flesh" does not necessarily mean that the view of marriage here involves a physical oneness; it may be taken to mean a oneness of human personalities.

Whatever the original meaning of Genesis 2:24, it is quite clear that the modern Christian needs to understand the passage to mean more than a physical unity in sexual intercourse. How then are we to understand this union of two personalities in marriage? We have spoken of it as a spiritual marriage or union, but what precisely does that mean? We suggest that the following may form the skeleton of a concept of marital oneness (it uses the language and thoughts of the twentieth century but remains true to the Biblical view of marriage).

1. The spiritual oneness of marriage is both a divine gift and a human achievement. This is to say that we cannot conceive of the uniting of two human personalitites as a strictly human accomplishment, for it is far too complex to suppose that such is the case. But neither can we pretend that this spiritual unity is simply the act of God without human cooperation. It defies realism to assert that the unity of marriage is bestowed as a gift from the heavens. On the contrary, it involves both the divine gift in a pair of lives and the diligent efforts of those two persons. We want to suggest that the spiritual unity of marriage comes in a paradoxical manner like the one Paul spoke of: "You must work out your own salvation in fear and trembling; for it is God who works in you, inspiring both the will and the deed, for his own chosen purpose." (Phil. 2:12, NEB) One's

salvation, Paul said, involves both divine act and the human act; similarly, we argue, true marital union results from human cooperation with divine action. Perhaps it seems a cop out to argue this way. But it appears that there are two inescapable dimensions to the uniting of a man and a woman in marriage: There is the dimension of their own human personalities—their compatibility—and their determination to fit their lives together. But there is also a dimension less explainable—a dimension of grace which seems to make itself present not simply as a result of human characteristics and efforts. So we must maintain that the spiritual union of a marriage is paradoxically *both* a divine gift and a human achievement.

2. The spiritual oneness of marriage is a dynamic process, not a static quality. The unity of marriage is not a state which is suddenly and miraculously experienced in the lives of two people. Nor is it a state which once achieved can never be lost again. Such romantic notions of marriage have been far too powerful in American society. The unity of the two personalities is a quality of interrelatedness that is nurtured in degrees. It is experienced to some degree, only to be lost, then to be restored still more strongly. It is a process that can be nurtured rapidly or diminish just as rapidly. It is never "achieved" or "possessed" in the sense that an object may be in one's possession. It is an elusive, delicate, always-changing relationship.

3. The spiritual oneness of marriage is the experience of shared personhood. In those few intense moments of oneness in marriage the couple senses that their respective personhoods are freely and fully shared. This means that marital oneness depends upon a good many features which we usually think of as "secular" but which have immense spiritual value: common life goals, compatible emotional features, shared activities, mutual respect, and open honesty (these are only a few). As they are nurtured, these features contribute to a growing sense of commonality and sharedness. As a couple develops these common features, their relationship takes on unity.

4. But the unity of marriage is always the mutual interpenetration of two independent individual personalities. To state it in the negative, the unity of marriage is never the absorption of one personality into the other. The oneness of the spiritual marriage does not destroy the individuality of either or both of the partners. An understanding of marriage informed by the disciplines concerned for mental health will

necessarily insist that both persons in a marital unity must maintain
their own individual integrity. Otherwise, the unity would be an
annihilation of one personality by the other. Again, we must resort
to paradoxical language: The unity of marriage is the oneness of two
persons in their continued individuality. We like to symbolize this
paradoxical characteristic of marriage with the figure eight laid on its
side.

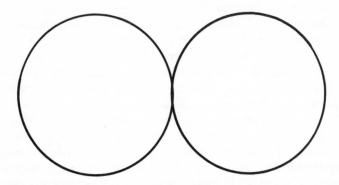

Viewed one way, the figure eight is composed of two independent
circles touching one another. Viewed another way, the figure eight is
one continuous, unbroken line. We believe that true oneness in marriage involves maintaining both the individuality and the unity of the
persons.

Surely this brief sketch of the meaning of marriage as a spiritual
union is grossly inadequate. But some such formulation as this should
be the heart of any statement of a Christian view of marriage. The goal
of spiritual oneness in marriage needs to be described in terms that
are both theologically and psychologically sound. Such a rethinking
of the view of marriage is the first and most vital step the church can
take toward implementing a new ministry to divorced and remarried
persons.

The second step is for the church to begin more vigorously to
teach this newly formulated view of Christian marriage. Through
preaching and counseling the pastor could give expression to where
the church stands on marriage. Marriage study groups might encourage both married couples and those anticipating marriage to think
through their relationships in the light of the Christian faith. Young

people in the church should be invited to study the concept and the institution of marriage in their classes and fellowship groups. Hence the educational program on this theme could reach through all the ages.

But a warning is necessary. It is our conviction that the church's educational ministry on marriage should be carefully tempered with realism. Too often the study books on marriage, the preaching on the subject, and the official statements of the church lack a basic realism. The Christian view of marriage is too often articulated in such a way as to sound like unattainable idealism. Let the church confront and take seriously that marriage is difficult, that every marriage has its moments of tension and strain, and that marriage is a life task to be worked at from beginning to end. In this way the church can identify with the real life struggles of married persons, and its teachings will take on a dimension of credibility.

The church needs to nurture within itself a new view of divorce and remarriage in the light of grace. If the conditions described in the little story of Janice that introduced our study are to be avoided, the church should aggressively seek to alter the attitude of people toward divorce and remarriage. This is indeed a long-term and difficult mission. The prejudices church members hold against divorced and remarried persons are in some cases deeply rooted. We have based our entire study on the assumption that some of those prejudices are grounded upon inadequate understandings of the Biblical materials and a deficient theology. That is surely the case with many church members. They are sincere Christians who wish to hold attitudes toward divorced and remarried persons which are soundly Biblical and theological. We hope that the kind of study we have done will enable many of these persons to comprehend a more Christian attitude toward the asundered of our society.

But realism necessitates that we recognize the other bases for prejudice against the divorced and remarried. One of those bases is surely emotional. Divorce arouses within many persons very deep and complicated feelings. The divorced person often finds that others respond to him or her in strange ways. It seems that the reactions of others to the fact of divorce are sometimes founded on a certain sense of insecurity. One divorced person had a long and serious talk with a couple who had been friends for many years. This couple finally in

honesty admitted that the divorce of their good friend was terribly
threatening to them. "If it can happen to you and Susan," they
confided, "it can happen to us." Many married couples will be threatened and frightened by the presence of a divorced person in their
midst. Their reluctance to accept that person will express not a theological or Biblical deficiency but an emotional insecurity. The pastor
and the enlightened lay person will need to be ready to discuss this
reluctance with skill and with the utmost love and concern.

Often the presence of a divorced person stirs deep memories and
old hurts. People may be reminded of the painful experience of the
divorce of their parents. Older couples may find the presence of a
divorced person an occasion to recall the bitterness and hurt of the
divorce of a son or daughter. Still other married couples may be
reminded of a stage in their own marriage at which they almost
decided to separate. All these complicated and profound feelings are
involved in the agonizing process of adjusting attitudes toward divorced and remarried persons.

But we have found still another group of people in the church.
They are not prejudiced against divorced and remarried individuals.
They have no deep, complicated emotions connected with divorce.
They simply do not know how to relate to one who has just experienced (or is in the process of experiencing) divorce. What do you
say? If you know both partners, how do you relate to one without
implying rejection of the other? These persons need the guidance of
the church just as much as the others mentioned above. They need
the reassurance that divorced persons have only the same basic needs
of all humans. They need to be assured that they can relate as friends
to both of the spouses of a broken marriage.

The community of faith might well look to its own needs and its
own shortcomings with regard to divorced and remarried persons. It
needs to nurture itself to be more accepting and loving. The light of
grace must brighten this blind spot experienced by so many devout
and mature Christians. The story of Jesus and the woman taken in
adultery (John 8:1-11) can help. (It is doubtless not a part of the
earliest form of the Gospel, but still it reflects an image of Jesus which
is entirely consistent with the one we find in the four Gospels.) Jesus'
attitude is not one of condemnation, but acceptance and forgiveness.
Nor is there a tone of condescension or self-righteousness in his

5 M 405

words. The sinner is accepted and forgiven though the sin is not condoned. Grace prevails over judgment. There is no one righteous enough to cast the first stone except Jesus and he will not. This passage can open doors of insight for the church's ministry to divorced and remarried persons.

The adjustment of attitude is a process that is long and difficult. Those who guide this process must be sure first of all that their own attitudes are straight. But if the Christian faith promises anything, it is that persons can change, that perspectives and attitudes can be altered, and that the Christian possesses a freedom from the dead weight of past prejudices.

The church needs to articulate the themes of forgiveness, redemption, and rebirth for the divorced. Many persons who are in the process of divorce or who are recently divorced are burdened with a sense of guilt. Of course, there is a great variety of reactions to the experience of divorce, and we must be careful not to stereotype the divorced person and what she or he is feeling. But often, especially among those who have been related to the ministry of the church, the divorced person is a guilt-ridden individual. And there is every reason for this. Divorce is a tremendous experience of failure. One of the most important tasks of life has been boggled. Divorce, moreover, is closely similar to the process of bereavement. All of the experiences of loss and fear that accompany the death of a loved one are often present in the life of the divorced. And the guilt that comes with the death of a loved one is also similar to the guilt that accompanies divorce. All of the regrets and second thoughts that come with any separation come with divorce.

The church needs to understand, we think, that in most cases divorced persons do not need to be told that they are guilty. All of the values which most divorced persons hold cry out condemnation. Society in general acts toward divorced persons with judgment and condemnation. Parents, friends, and children may well imply judgment in the way they react. The church need not add its voice of condemnation to the chorus already shouting "guilty" at the divorced. The church must instead offer a different and more constructive message.

And that message is one of forgiveness, redemption, and rebirth. Along with guilt, divorced persons also very often feel that life is opening up new opportunities. They feel as if they are starting over once again in life with all of the hopes and promises, as well as the fears and uncertainties that that new start involves. As a matter of fact there is ample evidence that people recently divorced often revert to the kind of activity and attitudes typical of their premarital life. Their life-style sometimes appears to be a sort of "second adolescence."

We say all of this because we believe the divorced person is often in a position to hear and understand the message of forgiveness and the promises of redemption and rebirth. They can identify with the need to be forgiven. They want a fundamental kind of forgiveness, the kind that comes from specific persons but which suggests that it is the Ultimate Reality of the universe that is offering forgiveness. They can identify with the promise of rebirth, too, because they sense that their own lives are on the verge of a new beginning. True, they may very likely be unable to articulate all of this. Most especially they may not be able to articulate it in religious terms. They may be inclined to think of their needs and feelings as having little to do with theological statements. But when the relationship is articulated for them, they may be able to appropriate it for themselves.

Divorced individuals often feel that their identity is up for grabs. They have defined themselves for years through the handy roles offered by society to the married. They have been husband or wife. They have participated in that great American dream of the house, the cars, the children, the job, the yearly vacation trips, and all the rest. Now suddenly all of that is gone. They are now misfits. They cannot really take their place alongside the single young adult any longer or the never-married group of adults. They are haunted by the fact that they were once married, so that they are neither fish nor fowl. In this couple-oriented society of ours, they do not belong. (See the study book *It's O.K. to Be Single,* ed. Gary R. Collins [Waco, Tex.: Word Books, 1976].)

The church's message of love and acceptance, of forgiveness and care, of redemption and rebirth can enable the divorced person to begin to reshape his or her identity once again. The church should not hesitate in its declaration that divorced people are, along with all Christians, forgiven sinners. Their identity can begin to take shape around the fundamental belief that the Christian is first of all a child of God, adopted by the Father into a new and promising relationship.

This relationship is well demonstrated in the familiar story of the prodigal son (Luke 15:11-32). The prodigal son was lost and in rags. As a sinner in rags he returned to his father and was loved, forgiven, and bestowed with riches. As Christians we must learn that we are clothed with the dignity of Christ; our robes of dignity are given to us by the grace of God. That same robe of dignity is worn by all Christians, including those who have suffered divorce.

The church needs, however, to offer concrete forms of forgiveness *and acceptance to the divorced.* The story of Jesus' healing of the leper in Mark 1:40-45 certainly illustrates that for Jesus there was no social tradition or custom that was more important than God's love and that love was expressed to a social outcast by a personal touch. In the act of stretching out his hand Jesus communicated God's love.

The church needs also to be willing to stretch out its hand to the divorced person. Words help, but they are not enough. Therefore, divorced persons will look inevitably to the program of the church to test the credibility of the words of grace spoken to them. They have a variety of needs. The program of the church can help to fill some of those needs. And to the degree those programs are relevant to the divorced person he or she will sense that the words of forgiveness, redemption, and rebirth are genuine. Maybe the first service the church can offer is a means of celebrating the occasion of the dissolution of marriage. More and more the church has begun to venture into the area of liturgies for the dissolution of marriage, and we believe that that may have some promise for the ministry of the church to divorced persons. It must be a semiprivate service, much as the wedding service is. It can be a time of sorrow and repentance as well as a time of rejoicing and forgiveness. The pastor should take the initiative in offering the service to those divorced persons she or he counsels. (See *Ritual in a New Day: An Invitation* [Nashville: Abingdon Press, 1976].)

But the divorced person has a multitude of needs that are more substantial. We cannot pretend the expertise to list the whole variety of needs there may be; but there is now a large literature on divorce, and we urge you to look into it (e. g., Russell J. Becker, *When Marriage Ends* [Philadelphia: Fortress Press, 1971]). But generally there are practical, emotional, and spiritual needs in the lives of many divorced persons. There is often a tremendous sense of loneliness. The church can help. It may want to develop a series of services to divorced persons in its midst. Perhaps these programs are best done as an ecumenical cooperative enterprise. There may need to be a special group for divorced persons. Perhaps another group for the special needs of single parents.

All of this is not proposing that the church become a social service agency for the divorced person. It may not have the expertise for that. But what is important to note is that the church must make its message of forgiveness and acceptance of divorced persons concrete. The way it does that best is through its programs. Those programs are then part of the Christian proclamation of grace. They are not distortions of the church's mission but concrete embodiments of that mission. They are means by which the church can stretch out its hand to the social outcast.

insone

 The church needs to facilitate remarriage as a means of rebirth. Here we must be careful not to imply that all divorced persons want to remarry. Their freedom to refrain from another marriage must be honored in every possible way. But for those who do desire to remarry, the church needs to be ready and willing to assist.

The first task of the church on this score is to present the possibility of remarriage as one symbol of rebirth. It might present remarriage as the second chance for the divorced person. The poignant symbols of death and resurrection are applicable here. The first marriage is dead, and with it have died the hopes and dreams of the individuals involved. But there may be a resurrection. God brings life out of the death of marriage. That life may take the form of remarriage. The church, we are saying, has at its disposal a powerful set of symbols by which to support the divorced person's desire to start again in a marriage relationship. The church can demonstrate that the power of God's grace overcomes the judgment that remarriage after divorce is adultery. It can nurture the belief that whatever sin has occasioned the death of the first marriage and whatever wrong may be found in the difficulties of building a new one, God's promise of grace prevails.

This means concretely that the pastor and able lay persons must do some effective counseling. This counseling can help the divorced person face marriage again with hope and strength. It can help them take the step of another marriage with the assurance that the church is there to support and nurture the marriage to the success which the first one failed to achieve. This may mean, too, that the second marriage needs to be sanctioned by the church in a special way. Again, there are some experimental liturgies being developed that are designed to be used with wedding celebrations of divorced persons. (See the brief proposal made by Dwight Hervey Small, *The Right to Remarry* [Old Tappan, N.J.: Fleming H. Revell Co., 1975], pp. 185-186; and *Ritual in a New Day* [Nashville: Abingdon Press, 1976], pp. 82-96.) Some divorced persons will want to use such a service for their wedding, and again the pastor needs to be ready to take the initiative to offer such.

We may be guided by Paul's reminder that with our baptism we have experienced a death and resurrection:

> Have you forgotten that when we were baptized into union with Christ Jesus we were baptized into his death? By baptism we were buried with him, and lay dead, in order that, as Christ was raised from the dead in the splendour of the Father, so also we might set our feet upon the new path of life. [Rom. 6:3-4, NEB]

We would like to think that Paul was wise enough to know that this was true not just of that one period in our lives when we embrace the faith and are baptized. The Christian life is a continuous dying to sin and the law only to be raised to new life in Christ. Our baptism is a symbol of that ongoing process of dying and rising. The community of faith is the support group which enables the process of being ever anew resurrected to faith and freedom. The community can, if it will, facilitate that process with regard to divorced persons who desire to be remarried. It can support the acceptance of the death of the past and the resurrection of the individual to a new opportunity for marriage. It can encourage the individual to understand the failure of one marriage and the opportunity of another as concrete expressions of the demise of old patterns and old difficulties and the emergence of new patterns and new joys.

The aim of these concrete proposals is that the asundered of our society might be reconciled—reconciled to God, the church, and to self. The ministry of the church must facilitate that reconciliation. It is a reconciliation which begins with the assurance that there is a reconciled relationship with God through Christ available to those divorced persons who will accept it. But it goes beyond a reconciliation with God. If the church can effectively communicate the fact of the reconciliation with God, it can also—as a community of faith—live a reconciled relationship with the divorced person. It can offer concrete acceptance, love, and understanding. The result will be a third dimension of reconciliation. The divorced person will thereby become reconciled with him or herself. With the assurance of God's forgiveness and acceptance and with the experience of actual acceptance by the members of the community of faith, divorced persons can come to grips with themselves. They can be led into a new self-acceptance and self-esteem, so vital to their well-being. The church can reconcile the asundered, and thereby it can act more fully as the body of Christ in the ministry of reconciliation.

BIBLIOGRAPHY

Chapter 1. Moses' Permission

Carmichael, Calum M. *The Laws of Deuteronomy.* Ithaca, N. Y.: Cornell University Press, 1974.

Danby, Herbert, trans. and ed. *The Mishnah.* London: Oxford University Press, 1933.

De Vaux, Roland. *Ancient Israel.* Vol. I: "Social Institutions." New York: McGraw-Hill Co., 1965.

Driver, S. R. *The International Critical Commentary: A Critical and Exegetical Commentary on Deuteronomy.* Edinburgh: T. & T. Clark, 1965.

Moran, W. L. "Deuteronomy." In *A New Catholic Commentary on Holy Scripture.* Ed. R. C. Fuller *et al.* Camden, N. J.: Thomas Nelson and Sons, 1969.

Murray, John. "Divorce: Deuteronomy 24:1-4." *The Westminster Theological Journal* 9 (1946): 31-46.

Paterson, John. "Divorce and Desertion in the Old Testament." *Journal of Biblical Literature* 51 (1932): 161-170.

Phillips, Anthony. *Deuteronomy.* Cambridge: University Press, 1973.

Pritchard, James B., ed. *Ancient Near Eastern Texts Relating to the Old Testament.* Princeton, N. J.: Princeton University Press, 1950.

Von Rad, Gerhard. *Deuteronomy: A Commentary.* Philadelphia: The Westminster Press, 1966.

————. *Studies in Deuteronomy.* London: SCM Press, 1953.

Yaron, Reuven. *Introduction to the Law of the Aramaic Papyri.* Oxford: Clarendon Press, 1961.

Chapter 2. But I Say unto You

Abrahams, Israel. *Studies in Pharisaism and the Gospels.* New York: KTAV Publishing House, Inc., 1967.

Bultmann, Rudolf. *The History of the Synoptic Tradition.* New York: Harper & Row, 1963.

————. *Jesus and the Word.* New York: Charles Scribner's Sons, 1935.

————. *Theology of the New Testament.* New York: Charles Scribner's Sons, 1951.

Cohen, A., ed. *Everyman's Talmud.* New York: E. P. Dutton, 1949.

Coiner, H. G. "Those 'Divorce and Remarriage' Passages (Matt. 5:32; 19:9; 1 Cor. 7:10-16) with Brief Reference to the Mark and Luke Passages." *Concordia Theological Monthly* 29 (1968): 367-384.

Grant, F. C., trans. and ed. *Form Criticism.* Chicago: Willett, Clark & Co., 1934.

Hiers, Richard H. *Jesus and Ethics.* Philadelphia: The Westminster Press, 1968.

Lehmann, Manfred R. "Genesis 2:24 as the Basis for Divorce in Halakhah and New Testament." *Zeitschrift für die Alttestamentliche Wissenschaft* 72 (1960): 263-267.

Mahoney, Aidan. "A New Look at the Divorce Clauses in Matthew 5:32 and 19:9." *The Catholic Biblical Quarterly* 30 (1968): 29-38.

Major, H. D. A.; Manson, T. W.; and Wright, C. J. *The Mission and Message of Jesus.* New York: E. P. Dutton, 1938.

Marshall, L. H. *The Challenge of New Testament Ethics.* London: Macmillan and Co., 1947.

Montefiore, C. G. *The Synoptic Gospels.* Vol. I. London: Macmillan and Co., 1909.

Olsen, V. Norskov. *The New Testament Logia on Divorce.* Tübingen: J. C. B. Mohr, 1971.

Perrin, Norman. *The New Testament: An Introduction.* New York: Harcourt Brace Jovanovich, 1974.

Richards, H. J. "Christ on Divorce." *Scripture* 11 (1959): 22-32.

Shaner, Donald W. *A Christian View of Divorce.* Leiden: E. J. Brill, 1969.

Taylor, Richard J. "Divorce in Matthew 5:32; 19:9." *The Clergy Review* 55 (1970): 792-800.

Taylor, Vincent. *The Formation of the Gospel Tradition.* London: Macmillan and Co., 1935.

———. *The Gospel According to St. Mark.* London: Macmillan and Co., 1952.

Von Rad, Gerhard. *Old Testament Theology.* New York: Harper & Row, 1962.

Chapter 3. The Lord's Ruling

Bornkamm, Günther. *Paul.* New York: Harper & Row, 1969.

Bultmann, Rudolf. *Existence and Faith.* New York: Meridian Books, 1957.

Conzelmann, Hans. *1 Corinthians.* Philadelphia: Fortress Press, 1975.

Craig, Clarence T. "I Corinthians, Exegesis." *The Interpreter's Bible.* Vol. 10. New York: Abingdon Press, 1953.

Davies, W. D. *Paul and Rabbinic Judaism.* London: S. P. C. K., 1948.

Furnish, Victor Paul. *Theology and Ethics in Paul.* Nashville: Abingdon Press, 1968.

Héring, Jean. *The First Epistle of Saint Paul to the Corinthians.* London: Epworth Press, 1962.

Moffatt, James. *The First Epistle of Paul to the Corinthians.* London: Hodder and Stoughton, 1951.

Murray, John. "Divorce: I Corinthians 7:10-15." *The Westminster Theological Journal* 10-11 (1947-1949): 168-191.

O'Rourke, John J. "A Note on an Exception: Mt. 5:32 (19:9) and 1 Cor. 7:12 Compared." *The Heythrop Journal* 5 (1964): 299-302.

Roberts, R. L., Jr. "The Meaning of *Chorizo* and *Douloo* in I Corinthians 7:10-17." *Restoration Quarterly* 8, no. 1 (1965): 179-184.

Robertson, Archibald, and Plummer, Alfred. *A Critical and Exegetical Commentary on the First Epistle of St. Paul to the Corinthians.* New York: Charles Scribner's Sons, 1911.

Roetzel, Calvin J. *The Letters of Paul: Conversations in Context.* Atlanta, Ga.: John Knox Press, 1975.

Tannehill, Robert C. *Dying and Rising with Christ.* Berlin: Alfred Töpelmann, 1967.

Whiteley, D. E. H. *The Theology of St. Paul.* Philadelphia: Fortress Press, 1964.

Chapter 4. The Asundered Reconciled

Becker, Russell J. *When Marriage Ends.* Philadelphia: Fortress Press, 1971.

Cantor, Donald J. *Escape from Marriage.* New York: William Morrow and Co., 1971.

Collins, Gary R., ed. *It's O.K. to Be Single.* Waco, Tex.: Word Books, 1976.

Doherty, Dennis J. *Divorce and Remarriage: Resolving a Catholic Dilemma.* New York: Abbey Press, 1974.

Emerson, James G., Jr. *Divorce, the Church, and Remarriage.* Philadelphia: The Westminster Press, 1961.

Hordern, William. *Living by Grace.* Philadelphia: The Westminster Press, 1975.

Krantzler, Mel. *Creative Divorce.* New York: New American Library, 1973.

Ritual in a New Day: An Invitation. Nashville: Abingdon Press, 1976.

Shepherd, A. P. *Marriage Was Made for Man.* London: Methuen, 1958.

Sinks, Robert F. "A Theology of Divorce." *The Christian Century* (April 20, 1977): 376-379.

Small, Dwight Hervey. *The Right to Remarry.* Old Tappan, N. J.: Fleming H. Revell Co., 1975.

INDEX OF BIBLE REFERENCES

INDEX OF NAMES AND SUBJECTS